SCHEMING PAPISTS
and
LUTHERAN FOOLS

SCHEMING PAPISTS
and
LUTHERAN FOOLS

Five Reformation Satires

Selected and Translated by

ERIKA RUMMEL

Fordham University Press
New York
1993

Library of Congress Cataloging-in-Publication Data

Scheming papists and Lutheran fools : five Reformation satires /
translated by Erika Rummel.
    p. cm.
    Includes bibliographical references and index.
    Contents: The powers of Rome — Lamentations of obscure men
(extract) / Ortvinus Gratius — Theologists in council / Crotus
Rubianus — The great Lutheran fool / Thomas Murner — A journey for
religion's sake / Erasmus.
    ISBN 0-8232-1482-6 (cloth). — ISBN 0-8232-1483-4 (paper)
    1. Reformation—Sources. 2. Catholic Church—Controversial
literature. 3. Lutheran Church—Controversial literature.
4. Satire, Latin (Medieval and modern) 5. Satire, German.
I. Rummel, Erika, 1942–
BR301.S34   1993
887'.02080382—dc20   92-34382
                                                    CIP

Permission has been granted by Yale University Press for use of an illustration
from Ozment, *The Age of Reform, 1250–1550*, copyright 1980 by Yale University
Press.

Printed in the United States of America

CONTENTS

ABBREVIATIONS

Allen   Allen, P. S., et al. *Opus epistolarum Des. Erasmi Rotero-dami*. 12 vols. Oxford: Clarendon, 1905–1958.

ASD   Erasmus, D.*Erasmi Opera omnia*. Amsterdam: North-Holland, 1969—.

CWE   Erasmus, D. *The Collected Works of Erasmus*. Toronto: University of Toronto Press, 1974—.

Introduction

THE BATTLE between the reformers and the champions of the old faith was waged not only by preachers thundering from the pulpits, theologians facing each other in acrimonious disputations, and church authorities issuing censures and condemnations; there was also a supporting cast of writers who had no official role or designated authority and whose arsenal contained neither prooftexts nor syllogisms but barbs of satire. Unlike the carefully crafted scholarly controversies with their complex technical terminology, these ad hoc productions were addressed to a wider audience of educated laypeople and took a visceral rather than a rational approach to the religious question. Satire, a genre that requires finely honed language skills, was the preferred weapon of the humanists, who by and large sympathized with the reformers. In fact, the two groups were so closely associated in the reading public's mind that the earliest phase of the Reformation was sometimes interpreted as a quarrel between philologists and theologians, a manifestation of professional jealousies. Thus Erasmus claimed that the debates of his time were the result of antagonism between the faculties of Arts and Theology. The conflict, he said, was misrepresented by the theologians who were out to discredit students of literature by associating them with Lutheranism: "There are people who have long been the sworn enemies of humane studies . . . and try with remarkable ingenuity and great insistence to mix up language studies with the business of Luther."[1]

Philological and theological issues are certainly intermingled in what is perhaps the most famous satire of the sixteenth century: the *Letters of Obscure Men*, which was published anonymously in 1515. The work grew out of a controversy originated by Johann Pfefferkorn, a converted Jew, who denounced Hebrew books as tools of heresy and advocated their destruction. The emperor, whose authority had been invoked, sought the counsel of scholars. Johann Reuchlin, a prestigious Hebraist, defended Hebrew literature and received the universal support of humanists; the theological faculties of several universities, on the other hand, sided with Pfefferkorn. Cologne, under the leadership of the Dominican Jacob Hoogstraten, a member of the faculty and inquisitor of the region, became Pfefferkorn's most zealous champion. The controversy issued into a pamphlet war. In the end Hoogstraten cited Reuchlin before his inquisitorial court, but the scholar appealed his case to Rome. For a while he appeared to be victorious. Pope Leo X reversed Hoogstraten's judgment and imposed silence on him; however, a counter appeal by the inquisitor prolonged the case until the summer of 1520, when Reuchlin was once again condemned.

At the height of the controversy, in 1513, Reuchlin published a volume of letters written by fellow scholars in defense of his position. He entitled the collection *Letters of Famous Men*. In 1515 another volume appeared under the title *Letters of Obscure Men*. At first glance it was a collection of epistles supporting Pfefferkorn and addressed to Ortvinus Gratius, a theologian at Cologne (see below, p. 48). On closer inspection, however, it turned out to be a hoax calculated to ridicule the anti-Reuchlinists. The fictitious letters, written in atrocious Latin and portraying the writers as fools and scoundrels, were put together in the humanistic camp. Among the authors were Crotus Rubianus (see below, p. 55) and Ulrich von Hutten, who politicized the religious struggle, pouring out a flood of pamphlets in the name of "German liberty" and finally advocating armed resistance against the clergy. Hutten's propaganda pieces were eagerly read in his own time, but fell into oblivion after his death, whereas the *Letters of Obscure Men,* with their timeless wit and humor, became a literary classic.

Another sixteenth-century satire, Erasmus' *Praise of Folly*, enjoys similar status and continued popularity. It remains the best-known work of the Dutch humanist, although it was no more than a *jeu d'esprit* dashed off on the spur of the moment and cannot compare in scholarly distinction with his edition and annotation of the New Testament or in social significance with his essays on politics and education. The *Praise of Folly*, a speech put in the mouth of Dame Folly advertising her own qualities, mocks the foibles of humanity and in particular the conceit and hypocrisy of theologians, monks, and other representatives of the church. What has earned this lighthearted lampoon a place in Reformation history is its unexpectedly earnest conclusion. Juxtaposing the folly of the world with truly Christian folly, that is, guileless simplicity and trust in God, Erasmus gave his satire a programmatic thrust.

Equally brilliant was the work of Erasmus' younger contemporary François Rabelais, one of the most erudite and elusive writers of satire, whose *Gargantua and Pantagruel* is a theater of the absurd. Criticism of the church appears in it in many forms, but the description of the Abbey of Thélème, the dream-come-true of worldly monks and nuns, the counsels of the coarse and fun-loving Friar John, and Greatclod's exaltation of the Decretals have become *loci classici*.

These three works—*Letters of Obscure Men, Praise of Folly* and *Gargantua and Pantagruel*—no doubt epitomize the genre, but they illuminate only a narrow band in the spectrum of sixteenth-century satire. Testimony to the intellectual ferment that characterized the Reformation, satire flourished and yielded an abundant harvest. There is a rich crop of minor pieces that offer the same winning combination of instruction and entertainment as the classic triad. There are obnoxious exchanges between theologians and "poets" (as the humanists were called by their critics), lampoons that mock faculties wholesale, carnival skits that offer unbridled criticism of notorious individuals, and fanciful compositions of baffling scurrility. These irreverent pieces frequently appeared without author's or printer's name, but local and regional authorities concerned about hate-mongering soon moved to suppress them, passing laws prohibiting anonymous publications. Thus the productions were ephemeral. Indeed many are no longer extant and are known to us only from oblique references in contemporary literature.

It is the purpose of this anthology to bring some of the surviving (and undeservedly neglected) satires to the attention of an English-speaking audience. The reason for the obscurity of these works does not necessarily lie in their literary inferiority to the classic three, but rather in the specific nature of the issues tackled. Large sections of the *Letters of Obscure Men* and the *Praise of Folly* may be enjoyed as literature and demand no special knowledge from the reader, but the pieces assembled in this volume do require some annotation. Their humor cannot be appreciated without a knowledge of the issues at stake. This very feature—the topicality of the pieces—makes them such valuable sources for the student of sixteenth-century history. The classics appeal to readers because they offer a wisdom that transcends the ages and observations that are timeless; the satires chosen for this volume are period pieces and offer comment on specific historical issues. They are therefore highly instructive; at the same time the witty presentation of the issues, which becomes apparent to readers once they are aware of the historical background, makes them attractive reading.

Of the five texts selected here, only one—Erasmus' "A Journey for Religion's Sake"—has previously been available in English; the others are presented here in translation for the first time. The composition dates of the pieces span the years from 1517 to 1526, a short but significant period which saw the posting of the *Ninety-Five Theses*, the issuing of the papal bull *Exsurge Domine* and the Edict of Worms. It is a period in which the Reformation grew from a protest to a movement. The earliest piece in this collection, the anonymous skit *The Powers of the Romanists* attacks the corruption of the Roman curia and its representatives. A common complaint at the time, it was given new impetus by reports of the scandalous conduct of the papal legate to Denmark, Angelus Arcimboldus, who was caught double-dealing, lost the wealth he had fraudulently accumulated, and narrowly escaped being imprisoned for his intrigues. The dialogue highlights the plight of petitioners to the curia. Their pursuit of justice was encumbered by the system itself, which required the payment of hefty fees and involved the cost and inconvenience of traveling to the nearest court representative, thus putting justice out of the reach of common people. The problems inherent in the system were aggravated by the greed and corruption of those charged with administering the process. The skit has nationalistic undertones, revealing a deep-seated antagonism between German petitioners and Roman curialists. The chauvinism depicted here is representative of a general European desire for national churches independent of Rome, as evidenced in the emancipation of the Gallican church, in the bargaining of the Spanish crown for special privileges, and (though special circumstances attended this case) in the breaking away from Rome of the Anglican church.

The second text, which is an extract from Ortvinus Gratius' *Lamentations of Obscure Men*, brings to life the controversy surrounding Reuchlin, adding a counterpoint to the well-known *Letters of Obscure Men*.

The third piece, Crotus Rubianus' *Theologists in Council*, makes the reader privy to the backroom dealings of a consortium of dour theologians who are bent on the destruction of the "poets," a term under which they lump together anything that is unfamiliar and therefore suspect to them: patristic authors, students of Hebrew and Greek, writers of polished Latin, and reformers. The speakers in the dialogue include Reuchlin's persecutor Jacob Hoogstraten, Luther's implacable foe Johann Eck, and Erasmus' nemesis Edward Lee, who engaged in a drawn-out controversy with him over the New Testament edition. There are uncanny parallels between these fictitious minutes and the historical minutes in the records of the faculty of theology at Paris, where a few years later Noël Béda and his cronies engaged in a witch-hunt that resulted in an official censure of Erasmus' works and in the execution of the outspoken Louis Berquin, who had translated some of Erasmus' works into French.

The fourth satire, *The Great Lutheran Fool* by Thomas Murner, represents the Catholic point of view. Written in German and, in its unsophisticated and coarse humor, carrying on the tradition of Sebastian Brant's *Ship of Fools*, the skit questions the motives of the reformers, casting them as self-seeking agitators and disturbers of the peace. According to Murner, they criticized the wealth of the church to obtain a share in it themselves, they spoke out against celibacy to satisfy their own base desires, and they introduced new doctrines out of a lack of respect for tradition. Murner specifically attacks and criticizes two popular reformation tracts: Johann Eberlin's *Fifteen Confederates*, which may be described as the Protestant *Utopia* and suggests some of the social legislation and ecclesiastical policies eventually adopted by reformed cities; and the anonymous *Karsthans* (widely ascribed to Hutten), a German peasant's defense of Lutheranism. Murner also lashes out against the *Bundschuh*, peasant associations with ties to the reform movement, which fomented the unrest that characterized the mid-

'20s and resulted in armed resistance against lords in many places. The ensuing upheaval and bloodshed led to a strange meeting of the minds: Luther in effect came to share Murner's point of view, publishing a tract *Against the Murderous and Thieving Throngs of Peasants* in 1525.

The fifth piece in the collection is one of Erasmus' *Colloquies*, "A Journey for Religion's Sake." Erasmus was sympathetic to the Reformation in its earliest stages; he shared and indeed anticipated the complaints of the reformers concerning the abuses of the church. He did not, however, formally break with the Catholic tradition and paid lip service at least to the teaching authority of the church, couching his views in hypothetical terms rather than issuing definitive statements. In the colloquy he takes a stand on the issues of pilgrimage and the veneration of saints, practices that the reformers wanted abolished. Erasmus ridicules the gullibility of pilgrims and castigates the church for encouraging superstition in order to increase donations, but he rejects the iconoclastic movement and concedes an ancillary role to ceremonies in the promotion of piety and devotion.

With the exception of Murner's *Lutheran Fool*, the texts were all written in Latin, Europe's lingua franca. By using the vernacular Murner restricted the circulation of his piece to the German-speaking region, but at the same time expanded the social circles from which he could draw his readership. His prime motive in choosing the vernacular as his medium would have been to reach the *same* audience as the reformers whose works he attacked. And reformers were addressing an increasingly larger audience, turning from their initial recruits in the university community to the patricians, tradespeople, and artisans in the cities, and even to the peasants in the countryside. Many members of the urban middle class would have had some knowledge of Latin, but naturally read the vernacular with greater facility. The specific circumstances attending the publication of each piece are explained in the headnotes preceding the texts. The headnotes also provide pertinent biographical information about the authors, although we have limited knowledge about men like Ortvinus Gratius, Crotus Rubianus, and Jacobus Sobius, whose lives were only briefly illuminated by their involvement in the Reformation. Biblical and classical quotations, technical terms, sixteenth-century customs and institutions, and allusions to historical persons and events are explained in the notes at the end of each piece.

NOTE

1. *Ep.* 1716:34–37 (Allen).

1

The Powers of the Romanists

THIS DIALOGUE,[1] which was published without date or place, is a protest against the corrupt and mercenary practices of representatives of the papal curia. It shows the hardship suffered by the common man caught in the legal system of the church and the difficulties he faced in obtaining justice. The papal legate, one of the principal characters of the dialogue, is clearly modeled after an historical figure, the legate Angelus Arcimboldus, whose corruption was notorious. His scandalous conduct in Denmark and the subsequent events described in the dialogue took place in 1517, which gives us a *terminus post quem* for the composition of the text. Two other characters, Bruno, a servant, and Henno, a man from the country, are witness and victim of the abuses of the system. The author's programmatic concerns sometimes override his considerations for persona. Thus Bruno's comments are rather more sophisticated than is to be expected from a tailor's servant; the peasant Henno—no doubt named after the protagonist of Reuchlin's comedy by that title—likewise displays an unexpected degree of classical learning. His character moreover undergoes a transformation in the course of the dialogue. Initially cast in the role of the victim, he promises in the end to become a willing collaborator and advertiser of the legate's powers. The dialogue fluctuates between fine irony, earnest critical asides, and scenes of comic relief as, for example, in the early morning encounter between the petitioner and two carousing nuns.

The authorship of this lively dialogue is uncertain. It has sometimes been attributed to Ulrich von Hutten,[2] but without solid evidence. Perhaps credence should be given to the sixteenth-century scholar and physician Cornelius Agrippa, who in a letter of June 1520 identified the author as Jacobus Sobius. Sobius, a native of Cologne, obtained an M.A. and a doctorate in law from the local university and taught there until his death in 1528. He moved in humanistic circles, befriended reform-minded men like Count Neuenahr and Johannes Caesarius, and cast his support behind Reuchlin.[3] His publications include editions and translations of classical authors and a patriotic address to Charles V on the occasion of his election in 1519.

Cast: Henno, a man from the country
       Polypragmon, a businessman
       Bruno, a servant
       Bartolinus, a court official
       The Roman Legate

HENNO: Hey, there! Is Polyphemus home? Is my friend, the tailor, home?

BRUNO: Oh, it's our dear Henno. Hello! How's it going? How's your wife?

HENNO: All right, working away as usual. But where is your master?

BRUNO: At dinner.

HENNO: Tell him I'm here, would you? And that I need to see him.

BRUNO: What? Do you want to buy something from him?

HENNO: I'm going to buy something or other soon, and urgently need his advice on it—he won't have to do it free of charge. I've brought him a gift: twenty fresh eggs from my farm and this cheese, a Sunday treat.

Bribe Already [handwritten marginal note]

BRUNO: You've done the right thing, Henno, because no empty-handed visitor is welcome here. Go into the kitchen while I call the master. He is having dinner in the dining room upstairs, looking out on the Rhine and taking in the fresh air—Master!

POLYPRAGMON: What is it?

BRUNO: Henno of Gluvel is here. He is bringing you eggs and cheese and says he needs to see you as soon as possible. Would you come downstairs?

POLYPRAGMON: I'm coming, dear guest. Hello, Henno.

HENNO: Hello, Polyphemus.

POLYPRAGMON: Polypragmon's the name.[4]

HENNO: Beg your pardon. It's a difficult name. But, by Jove, Polypragmon, there is a favor I want to ask you, a matter in which I need your considered advice and help—please.

POLYPRAGMON: If I can give you any advice or help, go ahead and make use of it, Henno. What is it? Speak.

HENNO: Yes, but first tell those people to go away.

POLYPRAGMON: Leave. Go away. [To Henno] Speak, then.

HENNO: I've hardly got the nerve.

POLYPRAGMON: Don't be shy. Don't hold back. Speak up, I say; there is no danger here. If you want the wound attended to, you must uncover it.

HENNO: But first promise me to keep everything to yourself.

POLYPRAGMON: Do you put so little trust in me—me, who entrusts his affairs to you?

HENNO: I brought you eggs and cheese.

POLYPRAGMON: I know. But now to your business.

HENNO: You know Battus, my only son?

POLYPRAGMON: Of course. The one with the broad shoulders, ruddy face, beaked nose, and red hair—the finest lad in the county?

HENNO: That's the one. That scoundrel, properly soused in the dark wine of our neighbor, the innkeeper, and with love urging him on, climbed through the window and raped the daughter of my sister Elsa. When he saw that the girl was pregnant, he took off, fearing the "priests' devils," as they call the fiscals[5] here, deserting me, an old man, who cannot do the work on account of his age, and leaving behind his dear loving mother. If you have any advice that will restore the son to his father and mother, tell me, I beg you. Our parish priest advised me to give a little present to the fiscal to soften him, if possible. So I've brought with me in this bag two large capons, of which (he says) these men are very fond. Tell me, Polypragmon, are you acquainted with the fiscal and could you come with me and put in a good word on my behalf?

POLYPRAGMON: No, I'm not acquainted with him at all, or else I would do it gladly. But, according to your account, your son's crime is a serious one. Twenty gold pieces will hardly be enough to satisfy the fiscal.

HENNO: My God, twenty gold pieces!

POLYPRAGMON: If not forty.

HENNO: That's the end! I'd rather be dead. It'll come down to the wire![6] Even if I sold my land and all my household goods and my cottage itself, I could never scrape together that much. [He sobs.]

POLYPRAGMON: Don't cry. There is perhaps a way out. We'll go to one of the court officials here, whom I know. If there are men that are both perpetrators and counsels of crime, it's them. I know just the right man to approach. [To Bruno] Hey, you, Bruno, come here!

BRUNO: Here I am. What are your orders?

POLYPRAGMON: You know, at church today I spoke with that old man, who is one of the principal court officials?

BRUNO: Yes, I know, you mean that decrepit swindler and impostor, that bane of many men, who is in bad repute everywhere, but doesn't give a damn. I wish he had died a death worthy of his deeds at the time when they locked him up tight.

POLYPRAGMON: Do you know where he lives?

BRUNO: I do. If you have no other orders, I'll run ahead.

POLYPRAGMON: Ask him to wait for us at home, if it's convenient. I'll come in a little while with Henno.

BRUNO: I'm off.

[Henno is sobbing.]

POLYPRAGMON: Don't fret yourself to death. This man will give you the right advice.

HENNO: I wish he would! But I haven't got any money. I have eggs, I have chickens, even a cow, if he absolutely insists—but nothing more.

[Bruno returns.]

BRUNO: He says you're welcome, he is expecting you at home.

POLYPRAGMON: Let's go, Henno.

HENNO: I'm going, I'm going,[7] but I have no pluck left.

★   ★   ★

POLYPRAGMON: Good day, worthy and wise Bartolinus.

BARTOLINUS:[8] Good day to you too. Have you followed my advice today and completed your business with the notary?

POLYPRAGMON: Conscientiously.

BARTOLINUS: Then your case is in good shape.

POLYPRAGMON: That's not what my opponent says. But let me introduce you to Henno, my friend. He has come here with me to ask your advice. Please give him the benefit of your counsel.

BARTOLINUS: Since I am a judge, I am prevented by law from giving counsel. But if he can make a contribution, I'll oblige him for your sake.

POLYPRAGMON: He can give you eggs, cheese, butter, honey, capons, a goat, but he can't give you money.

BARTOLINUS: Since I do not have those goods, I must buy them with money. But what is it all about?

POLYPRAGMON: Henno, tell your story. You know the case better than I.

HENNO: I don't dare to speak before great men. You tell the story, I beg you. I'm too embarrassed and inexperienced.

POLYPRAGMON: All right, I'll tell the story. His son, Battus by name, under the influence of wine and love, had unlawful intercourse with his neighbor, who is related to him in the second degree of consanguinity.[9] As a result of the act, the girl became pregnant and he fled, fearing the fiscal. The father wants to make it safe for him to return.

BARTOLINUS: Ha! I can tell he has never been in Rome, where this is the least crime committed. But it would not be in the interest of the Roman curia if men of his kind visited Rome and came to know the moral standards there. Their absolutions would have to be sold for less. Even as it is, peasants are getting wise to what's going on, and to Rome's detriment, for the price of indulgences had to be lowered,[10] the authority of the pope is undone, and judges are no longer held in as high esteem as before. People now care little about the pope's thunder;[11] indeed everything that was once of great importance in Rome has now come to nothing. And that's the fault of those who gave everything into the hands of the Florentines,[12] so that the pope himself was left empty-handed on

[handwritten margin note: Rome]

[handwritten note at bottom: A rape of a cousin in Germany is a big scandal. In Rome, it's a minor misdemeanor.]

account of their avarice. Add to this the large number of cardinals that were created in one day,[13] who were not satisfied with a pittance, but bought and sold everything openly, so that even a blind mole could not fail to see and detest it. Even I cannot praise everything they are doing—but we must see how his son can be restored to him and be married to the girl he raped, and how this can be done legally and without infamy. There is an apostolic legate here, who a few years ago brought from Rome a huge heap of indulgences and privileges to fund the building of St. Peter's at Rome.

POLYPRAGMON: I know the man and his angel-faced companions,[14] a filthy sewer of a fellow with hands like a hawk and a face pale with hunger. Everyone hates him and his companions; everyone curses him for robbing Germany of money—a strange false apostle, who sells off all of Christ's members, all of Christ's blood, all of the Holy Spirit's grace, the whole treasure of the church, and who sells even what was never in his power or possession. When he no longer made a profit here, he became papal legate in Sweden and Denmark,[15] they say, but he was deservedly punished by the "barbarians," as they call them,[16] and deprived of all his engraved gold and silver[17] which he had extracted there and taken away with him. They say that he was blinded himself and his companions hanged—has this monster come to life again?

BARTOLINUS: Watch what you are saying about a Roman legate. He couldn't have come back to life because he was not dead. But some misfortune struck him, that's for sure. The Danish king[18] deprived him of his gold, silver, and all property, and kept him prisoner, accusing him of having executed his commission in bad faith, of pretending to bring peace but acting otherwise. And they say that his brother has taken his place and is being kept prisoner until he pays a ransom.[19]

POLYPRAGMON: I see. But, tell me, what is your complaint, how did this affect you?

BARTOLINUS: My complaint? I was already on my way back, having won numerous lawsuits, when the councilors of that king got a hold of me and most unjustly threw me into prison.

BRUNO [aside]: What's most unjust about it is that they didn't immediately offer you the whole Rhine to drink. Then we wouldn't have to pay the ferrymen for crossing back and forth.

POLYPRAGMON: But back to the legate: Has he really returned?

BARTOLINUS: You are asking? Can't you tell from the fact that privileges were posted recently?

POLYPRAGMON: No, by Hercules! Will we have new indulgences? For I think that's what I heard. I heard something about the Holy Spirit Hospital in Rome having collapsed because of age and buried the patients in the rubble, and so more money is needed from Germany since the money from the previous collection was spent on [St. Peter's] cathedral.

BARTOLINUS: That collection was made by another man, of the Franciscan Brethren, a man of exceptional holiness and devotion.

BRUNO: That holy man was found in Westphalia late one night in a brothel, without his cowl, dressed in silk, playing the Greek[20] with some whores; and let me tell you, master, that kind of devotion to God and those frequent prayers in the privacy of his bedroom have already given him callused knees. Of course he was only obeying the precept in the gospel[21] that tells us, if we want to pray, to do so in the privacy of our bedroom behind closed doors; and on account of his remarkable abstinence he has exhausted all his energy and is quite pale—that's the holy man he is!

POLYPRAGMON: You don't say!

BRUNO: It's true. Believe me.

POLYPRAGMON: Why don't we drive out such monsters, such pestilent plagues, and uproot this weed from Christ's garden by fire, sword, or some other forceful means?

BARTOLINUS: That wouldn't be convenient at all. I would endanger myself.

POLYPRAGMON: Are you yourself guilty then?

BARTOLINUS: Yes, and I fear I'm not the only one. The line-up is a long one. There are many men of this kind among us, if you are referring to those that Rome has sent here—although there are still a few good men among them, but very few.

POLYPRAGMON: Few and far between, I believe. But what is your position among them?

BARTOLINUS: If you are thinking of those in Rome, I'm like a gnat among elephants, but here, some say, I'm in first place, although I wouldn't make such claims for myself. Only this much I want to have said in my praise and indeed hope it's true: that I am never better than when I cause a great deal of trouble with lawsuits, and even though I'm eighty years old I'm sparring for a fight and I'm dying of boredom when there isn't enough material. No doubt, boredom brings on sickness and sickness death, so one must keep busy.

POLYPRAGMON: And what about the people who keep you busy in this fashion? What do they say? What do they do in turn?

BARTOLINUS: What do they say? What do they do? You're asking? Some call me a crook for slandering and maltreating many; some call me a fraud because I am an expert at forging wills; others call me sacrilegious because I fraudulently obtain papal dispensations among the Romans who are now thoroughly corrupted (the whole city can be bought, together with Christ himself, as that Numidian king once said).[22] Others stage a fight with me in court, but they get nowhere. I ignore them all. In my opinion, people who talk like that about me aren't my friends. I have learned that much in Rome, where everyone ignores his bad reputation for the sake of money or ecclesiastical office. As for those who oppose me, I rely on the help of my close friend, my God, and triumphantly defeat them.

POLYPRAGMON: With the help of God? Whose God?

BARTOLINUS: Don't ask. I have him shut up here in my seal ring, and he is prepared to act on my nod.

BRUNO [aside]: By the faith of God and men, does the church of Christ have such prelates, such priests? That is a new kind of Holy Spirit, different from the one through whom our apostles worked miracles. Has the devil succeeded God? [Aloud] Master, ho! The sun is setting. Henno wants to go home and asks you to speed up your meeting with the worthy Bartolinus.

BARTOLINUS: He won't be able to go home today. He must meet that papal legate I've mentioned. It's too late today. We must see him early tomorrow morning. And to give you easier access to him, I'll provide you with a letter of recommendation to His Paternity, so he won't ask too much for the absolution and dispensation which you need for the incest that has been committed and the marriage that is to be contracted.

HENNO: Yes, please, do so, sir, although I can't pay much.

BARTOLINUS: I'll look after your business well. But listen, I understand you have brought two capons with you? You must leave them here, for I am not in the habit of acting on clients' behalf for nothing. You must pay something. If you have no money, you must give something else. The apostles lived after the motto "give freely and receive freely,"[23] but not so the judges. The order of the day is different in the church now than it was then. In fact, if I hadn't brought some two thousand ducats with me to Rome, I wouldn't have had patrons and helpers and advocates and favorable judges. And that God of mine would have been no help if those golden servants had not accompanied him.

BRUNO: You describe yourself and those men well.

POLYPRAGMON: If you insist, he will give the capons to you, although I had hopes of getting them myself. Henno, give him the two capons you have with you.

HENNO: Well, take them, then.

BARTOLINUS: Henry, hey there, Henry! Come here and take these two capons from Henno, cut off their wings and see that they are properly dressed. By the way, Polypragmon, I must tell you, I have a problem: I had a loyal cook, who was neither slow nor lazy, but the wretched woman died and I'm really vexed because ever since her death my servants are dilatory in their services. They were more afraid of her, when she was alive, than of me.

POLYPRAGMON: May she rest in peace.

BARTOLINUS: Amen. Now just wait a little here, my friends, while I go in and write the letter that Henno is to deliver tomorrow. Have a seat in the meantime and I'll be with you in a little while. [Exit Bartolinus.]

POLYPRAGMON: What do you think of him, Henno?

HENNO: He has a peasant's face and a cunning mind. I think he sees a lot.

POLYPRAGMON: And he accomplishes even more.

BRUNO: That's true. He accomplishes a great deal and all of it bad.

HENNO: Is that what they learn in Rome?

BRUNO: That and more.

[Bartolinus returns.]

BARTOLINUS: I have written in a tone that is both friendly and official. The paper is a bit dirty and the letters a little wobbly. That's because I'm covered with scabs.[24] To be honest, I'm writing this request to do you a favor. But see that you are there early in the morning, Henno, so that you are the first one to see the legate. It will be to your advantage for many reasons but in particular because it will permit you to return to your home sooner.

HENNO: I'll do it without fail, but I don't know where he lives and I have never seen him before.

BRUNO: Master, if it's all right with you, I'll bring him there. I know the man and where he lives. Also, if necessary, I can speak for Henno. At the same time I hope to learn something that is of advantage to me as well as to you. Henno is used to country ways; he doesn't know how to act before men of that kind. He won't understand what's going on—their practices, as they call them. And when they see him coming on his own, they'll treat him as they please and play tricks and have fun with a country bumpkin, whether or not he has a letter from Bartolinus.

POLYPRAGMON: You are a good fellow, and smart. By all means go with him. But make sure you don't miss a word the legate says, for I hear he is a clever fellow.

BRUNO: I'll make sure. Do you need me for anything else?

POLYPRAGMON: No, thanks. [To Bartolinus] Farewell.

BRUNO: Fareill. [sic]

HENNO: Farewell.

BARTOLINO: My regards to your Ursula.[25]

HENNO: What's he saying? Is he cursing me, Bruno?

BRUNO: Don't you know? It's a malediction.

HENNO: I don't understand a thing. Let him go to Hell. As far as I can see, he is the worst scoundrel.

BRUNO [reciting]: "Hear, then, O Greeks, the tale of cunning and crime and learn from the woe of one man."[26] But you, Henno, be ready at dawn tomorrow and when we go to see that legate, look your best. Brush the dirt off your clothes, clean and polish your shoes, shave, comb your hair, wash your hands and face, and clip your fingernails—in short, see to it that you look like a man of the city, not like a peasant. Otherwise he'll regard you as a suitable victim for his tricks. He has eyes like a lynx.

HENNO: Good advice. I'll do as you say, even though among my people I am the judge. No one in our village surpasses me as far as good manners are concerned. Everyone says that I deserve to be council chairman in a wealthy city. After all I was brought up in this city almost from the cradle until puberty. I know the manners of city men. But I have never met an apostolic legate before. So you must tell me what I have to do, I beg you. It is an art to observe the protocol of first greetings. My neighbors always deliberate far in advance before addressing either me or the lord of the manor. That is how well ordered things are among us. That's how much respect there is.

POLYPRAGMON: Coming, Henno? You can sleep at my house. We'll make a bed for you. Don't go away.

HENNO: I am merely getting advice from Bruno here on how to conduct myself tomorrow. As for asking me to stay with you—I gladly accept.

BRUNO: When you come to the door [of the legate's house], you must call on God so that everything will go according to your wishes; then, when you see the legate himself, prostrate yourself and kiss his feet, and then put the letter of the worthy Bartolinus to your lips before you give it to the legate with these words: "Your Holiness, I present this letter as your humble petitioner."

HENNO: I always thought that one kisses only the pope's feet and calls only him "holy."

BRUNO: And the legate's too because he represents the pope. He is his legate, so it is fitting.

HENNO: Well, better to kiss his feet than his ass, especially if it's worthwhile.

BRUNO: His ass too, if you want, Henno.

HENNO: Shut your mouth; you talk too much. Polypragmon has already gone into the house. Let's get going and follow him. And let's go to bed immediately so that I can get up earlier tomorrow.

BRUNO: Tomorrow, when you see the sun rise and shine into your bedroom, call me because I have difficulties getting up in the morning.

HENNO: No need to ask, I would have done it on my own accord because I'm sure I won't sleep a wink tonight. Till tomorrow morning, then, my host Polypragmon, good night.

POLYPRAGMON: Goodnight to you too, Henno. But listen, before you go, ask for a sleeping draught to drink.

HENNO: No thanks, I'm going.

★   ★   ★

HENNO: Ho, Bruno. It's light already. Wake up.

BRUNO: Yes, yes, Henno, I'm getting up already. Sweet is sleep to those without a care. Have you cleaned up as I told you to yesterday?

HENNO: Of course. Don't you see? Look at my shirt and my boots and my face and my hair and my hands.

BRUNO: Great, Henno, take care that the women don't fall in love with you, when they see you.[27] In this city it's dangerous to be too handsome, you know.

HENNO: Don't talk nonsense. Would women fall in love with an old gray-haired man? I should be so lucky! Let's go.

BRUNO: I'm not holding you up.

pp. 20-25
Rome vs. Germany

HENNO: Which way do we go?

BRUNO: Do you know the building where the holy knight sits on his horse of stone?

HENNO: I know: we go straight ahead, then turn left at the narrow gate, then we come within sight of a large round tower, a monument of great antiquity, near the church.

BRUNO: That's where the legate is staying. I only wish it were elsewhere because he gives a bad reputation to both the house and its Lord.

HENNO: We are getting close. Look, there is the tower. I just hope it's not too early; it hasn't struck four yet.[28] By Jove, who are those veiled women coming hurriedly out of the legate's house? I could almost believe that there is a new competition among those three goddesses[29] to see who is the most beautiful, and since that Phrygian shepherd[30] is no longer around, they have consulted that apostolic judge in his dreams. A lovely dream, even if those girls aren't goddesses.

BRUNO: You think they are goddesses, Henno? You are wrong. Goddesses existed a long time ago, among the pagans. We don't believe in goddesses, according to our true religion.

HENNO: I made a mistake. Who are they then?

BRUNO: They are poor bedwrestlers,[31] who have received alms from the apostolic treasure because of their diligent nightwork. For the Romanists believe that the money of those barbarous Germans[32] can be turned to no more pious and holy purpose than to pay for those truly poor girls. And, let me tell you, all the money which for all these many years we have sweated for and made every effort to collect for indulgences that supposedly paid for the war against the Turks or for calling a council or building churches; all the money we sent to Rome for pallium fees;[33] all those myriads of ducats every single year for annates of benefices which are due on account of the agreements with the princes of Germany (the so-called concordats[34]—nothing more astute or pressing could have been devised by the Romans, they say); all the money they got together on account of all those bulls, supplica-

Germans paying for Roman misdeeds / waste.

tions, concessions, and privileges; all the money collected from kingdoms, potentates, cities, counties, and taxable subjects which they have extorted without mercy—all that money was spent on nothing but those poor girls, surely in the most holy fashion and in complete accord with the teaching of the gospel and the apostles.

HENNO: What you describe is the pilfering of the German nation! It's a miracle there's anything left.

BRUNO: That's what bothers them, that they haven't got it all.

HENNO: But, tell me, are women the only ones who get money, and is all this mercy poured on them alone?

pedophilia

BRUNO: On boys and men too, for they have read in the holy books that there must be no distinction of persons.[35] They call them their little friends.

HENNO: What would they do with men?

BRUNO: What would they do, you ask? What Jupiter once did with his catamite, Ganymede, whom he had delivered by his eagle from Troy—a matter that really upset Juno,[36] they say.

HENNO: Ah, I see. I've heard that the Florentines do that sort of thing. So they do it too? What a crime!

BRUNO: The Florentines are not the only ones addicted to this heinous crime; it is also committed among those in Rome who are conspicuous in their black and purple hats and robes with long trains.[37] I have heard that they brag of it so often at their parties that one might think it was no crime but an amusing and charming game. Indeed, they say that women are smelly in summer, whereas men are excellent for the purpose, and on account of such skills boys are promoted and become bishops and cardinals, the pillars of the church, from whom afterward the Supreme Pontiffs are elected.

HENNO: These are strange tales. Perhaps these aren't crimes for them and they are allowed to do what others aren't under any circumstances. Perhaps the sin depends on the place. I understand that they consider drunkenness a serious crime and cast it into our teeth as a great vice, whereas we think it's a laudable thing. If I came across people like them in my county, I would immediately condemn them to the stake, and would treat them no differently than those who committed bestiality. That is how totally we condemn this crime. But listen, as far as I know, the proverbial saying "the closer to Rome, the less Christian"[38] is not without truth; I have seen it in our own priests who return from Rome steeped in vice and who set a terrible example for us. On the other hand, they learn nothing that is conducive to piety or good morals either in word or in deed, and are ignorant of all things, even how to celebrate Mass or explain the gospel so that the common people might understand it. They are arrogant, quick-tempered, fond of drink, without self-discipline, violent, inhospitable, libidinous, gambling, bragging, and womanizing.

BRUNO: If they are put in charge of churches after having trained in that ring, how can they be any better than men who come to the altar of Christ from stables, brothels, and whorehouses (for that is what the schools of Rome are)? No wonder that our clergy is so wicked, if in Rome such men are leaders.

HENNO: I don't understand how these leaders can be at the same time wicked and holy.

BRUNO: It's none of your business to understand it; in fact, you are not even supposed to understand it, for in the gospel, too, Christ wanted some things concealed from the apostles, others from the wise men, others again from the unlearned people. No wonder, then, that a country bumpkin like you is ignorant of most things and unable to understand them even if it were permissible, for these things are not apparent even to the most prudent and best of mortals. That's why I wish I were in Rome. I am confident that I would understand all the secrets and tricks in a very short time, for I know that I have a fertile mind.

HENNO: Look, the veiled figures are coming toward us—well, aren't they elegant! I wouldn't mind having them, even on an empty stomach! Do you know them, Bruno?

BRUNO: I think they are holy virgins, the same ladies that the legate often invites to his parties.

HENNO: What? Nuns?

BRUNO: Does it surprise you that holy company joins with holy men and bad company with bad men? The food matches the lips,[39] as they say. They have done their nightly chanting and taken turns saying their precious morning prayers. But I couldn't swear to you that they are virgins. I am very peculiar in the matter of swearing.

HENNO: I wish I were the sacristan at their nunnery.

BRUNO: Quiet, peasant, that's like putting a dog in the bathhouse or a pig in perfume. Besides if you want such a job, you have to cover up your gray hair and your rustic manners. [To the women] Hi, there! Afraid of us?—They don't say anything.

HENNO: The holy must not speak to the profane, as far as I understand. I'll knock on the door. What the—it's open already. So let's go in. Bruno, go ahead, I'll follow.

BRUNO: Call on God, as I told you, Henno.

HENNO: I call upon you, God, the giver of all things. Let my meeting with the papal legate be successful. And I call on you, Peter and Nicolas, together with our most generous Martin and all the other saints in heaven; stand by me, grant me the happiness of returning to my house, wife, and family with my lost son redeemed. And in witness of my prayer I'll light three wax candles for you.—[To Bruno] But isn't that man I see there the legate, that squat fellow with the bull's face and the loud voice? It's as if a lion roared. I'll get down on the floor, as you told me.

BRUNO: No, don't. That's not the legate.

HENNO: I thought he was. Who is he then?

BRUNO: He is the relative of some greedy pope. They call him Bullshead.[40] He was sent by the Florentines to accompany the legate—just as keen-eyed Argus[41] was sent once by Juno to accompany the heifer Io[42]—to make sure no one steals anything of the pope's treasure (for they don't trust each other). Just listen, what he once did, Henno. By God, I must tell you the story. Call me a liar if I didn't hear it told by the most trustworthy authority when I served at the table of the master.

HENNO: I'd like to hear it. What's it all about?

BRUNO: The legate invited two women to dinner. They were respectable women, young and good-looking. When they had taken their place at table, he took his seat between the two Muses like some Apollo.[43] Since he could not converse with them because they didn't speak his language, he began to pay them attention with nods and gestures, and rather lewd gestures at that. When they turned away, disgusted by the man's bad manners, and he saw that he couldn't win them over with words, he tried a practical method. He took hold of the more beautiful of the two, took out from the depth of his folds his fat penis, which might have belonged to a horse, and slipped it into her hand. The woman, who had expected nothing of this sort, was stunned by this huge monster, and blushing deeply all over, snatched away her hand in fright, as if she had touched a snake.

HENNO: And the other guests? Did they notice? Did they not cover him with abuse, give him a thrashing, and throw him out?

BRUNO: Not at all. The guests were all Romans. They are used to that sort of thing and laughed it off. Only one, who was personally touched by the insult, was upset. The noble ladies all lowered their eyes and blushed, but no one said a word.

HENNO: That's a dirty business, by God. I would have had him publicly whipped and after cutting off one ear thrown him out of the county.[44] I would have punished that filthy wretch. But, tell me, Bruno, is the rest of the household of the Roman legate like this foul pimp?

BRUNO: Pretty well. And not only are they hated by the citizens for committing rape, adultery, and other crimes, sometimes they are even attacked with weapons.

HENNO: I am surprised the city council puts up with it. After all, the household clearly reflects the master. I hear that a philosopher once said that the citizens of a country are like their princes.[45]

BRUNO: So you've become a philosopher, Henno?

HENNO: Even if I'm not a philosopher, I know that much from experience. Hey, who is the man I see coming toward us, Bruno, that tall fellow in silk, with the round cap, looking like a bearded goat and carrying a lot of bulls in his hand? That must be the legate.

BRUNO: That's him. Now remember what I told you, Henno.

LEGATE [musing]: Too much worry, too many troubles, I can't get any rest at night or at any other time, to say nothing of that sickening affair in Denmark. And that nice morsel they snatched from my jaws vexes me[46]—bad luck all around! I've missed out on the archbishopric,[47] for which I laid my plans so neatly and which I practically had in my hands. I lost a lot of money—though that doesn't worry me too much since I can always get from some other source what I lost in that case, and since it was more the pope's loss than mine—about twenty thousand ducats which I had diligently collected from the Danes and Swedes for the building of St. Peter's (a project otherwise most fortunate for me). I barely got away myself. That barbarous king acted contrary to all international law in his treatment of me, and that after first receiving me most kindly and calling me an Angel of Peace[48] for coming to Denmark for no other reason than making peace among the barbarians and pacifying everything. And things were going so well with the sale of indulgences and the rest of the authorized privileges I had among the Danes, a simple and devout people. Even the king himself gave me a generous gift, worthy of himself and of the Supreme Pontiff. Lulled into security by this display of benevolence and friendship, I left for Sweden, delegating the Danish business to my dearly beloved brother, a citizen of Milan, who was with me. When I returned from Sweden where I had gone to settle the conflict and arrange for a treaty between the parties on conditions foul or fair, I realized that the king had changed in his attitude toward me and had turned into an enemy. As soon as I realized that something was going on, I made sure that the treasure I had collected from the barbarians was transported by one route, while I took another, and so I escaped unharmed, but the money was intercepted and my brother thrown into jail.

Afterward I obtained a copy of a letter from the king to the pope, in which he accused me of many crimes. And he no longer called me an Angel of Peace and Roman apostolic legate, but a rabble-rouser and wretched traitor. He called me so because I had used his enemies to force the archbishop of Uppsala, an excellent man and the king's supporter, to resign his archbishopric against his will and under duress, because I arranged to have seven hundred ducats paid annually over and above the income from the bishopric. To keep my fraudulent actions secret and cover up my ambition and avarice, I pretended that all of this was a spontaneous action of the Swedish tyrant, done under his own steam, as they say, without my knowledge and against my will. Furthermore, he said, I had accepted from his enemy three thousand ducats in unrefined silver and copper to expedite things (their way of speaking of bulls), to defend him and the Swedish rebels in Rome against the right and lawful king, and to buy myself the required number of cardinals to join me as champions and protectors of the Swedish cause. Next, he said, I was present and tolerated that the archbishop, that worthy and good man, was struck on the head by one of the followers of the tyrant and that I absolved the assailant from this sin. Next I cast the bishop together with his father, a worthy and illustrious knight, and other nobles into a most horrible jail, where they could entertain no hopes, while I in the meantime enjoyed my seven hundred fraudulently obtained ducats. He claimed furthermore that on top of this I had without justification demanded a papal ban against him and brought false criminal charges against him before the Swedes, violating diplomatic law and the spirit in which the pope had sent me as his legate. In the same letter he begged and besought the pontiff to bring the law down on me for being a traitor and faithless legate, or else he would be compelled to take things into his own hands. As for the rest which the king found out one way or another, I'm sure that none of my people betrayed me, because no one knew what I was up to except one or two very reliable people. However, I realize from the king's accusations that my letters must have been intercepted, for he says he can prove the whole matter on the basis of letters, and that has me really worried. And I don't know how I'm going to get out of that business other than by denying everything strenuously, a strategy that has proved very helpful so far. Consequently I'm not afraid of the vengeance of the pope. I even have hopes of extracting my imprisoned brother from the hands of the king, with the intercession not only of the pope but even of the neighboring princes.

As for the pope's instructing the bishops in the regions bordering on Denmark carefully to investigate the truth of the matter, I'll easily deal with that through bribes and prayers, especially if I stay here a little while until the affair dies down by itself, which is the advice some friends gave me. In the meantime I've achieved this much with the faithful help of the Florentines: I can make a decent living here and collect sums that are by no means negligible, so that I have been given the same powers as I had before, and more. Of course the advisers of the local bishop, hardened and spiteful men, have forbidden me to use these powers in the name of the archbishop and say that all my actions are fraud and deceit, that my only purpose is to deceive the Germans in any way possible and take them for their money, that I have everything for sale, honest or not, and ask for more than that Simon Magus did once, when he deposited his money at Peter's feet.[49]

I wish I had the powers Peter had:[50] the gift of tongues, the gift of healing, of cleansing the lepers, of reviving the dead, the spirit of prophecy, and the power to bestow the Holy Spirit through the laying on of hands. I would turn a better profit than that fellow Peter and his rustic apostles did then. They barely had enough to eat even though they possessed the means of making a great deal of money and gaining immense wealth. One could have rightly applied to them what Marhabal is reported to have said to Hannibal in the Punic War:[51] "The gods don't bestow all gifts on one man." The apostles knew how to win, but they had no idea how to make use of their victory. I on the other hand have nothing but an authorization on a piece of paper, nothing but the lightning of anathema[52] which is getting a bit dull by overuse, the power to dispense with apostolic discipline, to absolve men of perfidy and broken oaths, to override the decisions of sacred councils, crown the stupid, give away black hats, and many other things that everyone agrees is setting pernicious examples for the Christian commonwealth, and all that for the sake of money—but the people no longer care for these privileges and consider them worthless. Thus no one buys my wares and I shall be reduced to poverty. If I don't sell the whole merchandise for a good penny, I'm done for and can starve or hang myself.[53] [He catches sight of Henno and Bruno.] But wait, I'm saved. It looks like there are people here who want to buy something.

BRUNO: [aside] I heard and understood everything, nothing has escaped me. It's a tale of truly apostolic deeds. Paul's mission to the gentiles was nothing by comparison.[54] [To Henno] Prostrate yourself, Henno, won't you?

HENNO: [prostrate, to the legate] This humble petitioner presents this letter to his Holiness.

BRUNO: What a peasant! He's such a boor, he forgot to kiss the letter, as I told him. He can't change his rustic ways.

LEGATE: Rise. How is the worthy Bartolinus? Has he recovered from the mange yet? Such a good and industrious man does not deserve the injury and embarrassment which he unfortunately has suffered. And you—what is your name?

HENNO: Henno.

LEGATE: From the country, I suppose.

HENNO: Yes, I can't deny it.

LEGATE: What is your business?

HENNO: I am a farmer.

LEGATE: I see from the worthy Bartolinus' letter what your request is: that I absolve your son first of all from incest, since he had intercourse with a virgin related to him in the second degree of consanguinity, and secondly that I give him permission to marry the girl he raped—is that the gist of your petition?

HENNO: Yes.

LEGATE: Let me tell you about the nature of the petition you bring forward on behalf of your son. First of all, raping a virgin is a heinous crime, for which even secular laws order capital punishment. After all, he has taken away what not even God can restore. Then your son created a situation which makes it likely that she will have intercourse with others and finally earn money by prostituting her body. For a woman who has once tasted sweet pleasure is not likely to be able to abstain, and all subsequent sinful acts recoil on the rapist, the perpetrator of the first sex act. Secondly, there is the aggravating circumstance of a second degree of consanguinity, which you Germans more than any other people hold sacrosanct and inviolable. In fact, you condemn to the stake anyone whom you find indulging in this pleasure. Apart from the fact that such crimes demand harsh punishment, they would also set a pernicious example for you if they were absolved quickly and without thought. Therefore, if your son himself had sought impunity and forgiveness for this deed, he would have been obliged to go as far as Rome at great expense and even greater inconvenience. If in addition he is in love with her and doesn't want her to have intercourse with others but would rather marry her himself, that's also a matter of dispensation. You will understand this best if I give you the historical background on who was once allowed to do what with whom.

BRUNO: If Henno here cannot comprehend everything you say, I at any rate shall make sure that it is committed to memory.

LEGATE: According to ancient law, marriage among relatives was not only allowed, it was even forbidden to seek a wife outside the clan. Thus Nachor, Abraham's brother, married Melcha the daughter of his brother Aram. . . .[55] [Here the legate cites a long list of biblical precedents for marriage among relatives, which in his own time was, however, forbidden by church law.] . . . but since this law was instituted by man, it can be waived by man, that is, by the Supreme Pontiff, or, if he so wants, completely abolished and taken out of all law codes. For such is the power of the pope which has been transferred to me as through a channel, so that I can in his name do here what he can do in Rome. But because I am under financial constraint here on account of my large household and am in great need of money, I cannot give away the dispensation requested from me. There is a certain fee to be paid for each single document, to which I am entitled by papal decree. Therefore absolving your son from rape and incest and providing a papal dispensation so that he can marry her comes to forty ducats.

HENNO: Oh, no! Oh, no!

BRUNO: Now I see plainly what money can do. If you pay cash, it will do away with Christian charity and all natural and human decency. What next? This legate will remove all risk of sin so that nothing keeps us from abandoning ourselves to promiscuous sex like animals. Sons won't respect their mothers, nor fathers their daughters, brothers their sisters, or stepsons their stepmothers. We see that huge conflagrations arise from tiny sparks. We daily experience bad things getting worse and good things turning into bad, but we have yet to see evil being converted into good. Therefore I expected, in fact I was certain, that all this theological talk about the Old and New Testament[56] would add up to one thing: money is needed.

HENNO: By the immortal God, I'm done for. I'm as good as dead. What a wretch I am! That damned Battus, all the troubles he is getting me into, all the miserable pains he inflicts on his wretched father. I pay the legate forty ducats? I who haven't seen a ducat in forty years? And as I said yesterday, if I sold everything I have, including house and grounds which provide me and my family with a living, even if I sold myself into slavery afterward, the sum total wouldn't come to forty ducats.

BRUNO: What can we do, Henno?

HENNO: I don't know what to do. I'm totally ruined.

BRUNO: Let's get on our knees and beg him. Who knows, he may give us a discount.

HENNO: A discount is no good to me. I couldn't even give him the amount of the discount. I'm as good as dead!

LEGATE: I know those people. Even if they have plenty and are rich, they cleverly pretend to have nothing. Listen, Henno, your clothing, your cleanliness, your very face proclaims that you are a rich man.

BRUNO: It would have been better if he had come dirty. I gave him the wrong advice when I told him to come with clean clothes, boots, hands and face. Now this man thinks he found someone to milk—how wrong he is! [To the legate] Sir, this man has nothing, and you can verify that by sending your own investigators. The county in which he lives is not far away from this city. It's not a mile's distance.

LEGATE: But at least he can give twenty ducats—it's a great crime we are dealing with.

BRUNO: He couldn't even come up with ten gulden!

LEGATE: What, not even ten gulden? Then he's come in vain. I can't give away things for free because I don't get them for free. And even if I did and could give anything away, I don't see why an Italian should do a favor for a German and a man from the country at that.

BRUNO: Because he is a Christian and poor. You will get your reward in heaven.

LEGATE: I've pocketed heaven a long time ago and can sell it off any day at my discretion. Even Christ himself is in my power and obliged to do what I want.

BRUNO: What? Your Paternity can sell even Christ? I thought he had been sold once for all.

LEGATE: I don't sell him as that Judas did, who sold him by handing him over to the Jews to crucify. I sell him, but at the same time I hang on to him, which can be done without the sin of betrayal.

BRUNO: Wonderful! I wish my master knew this art so that he could sell clothes and hang on to them at the same time. Soon he would be richer than Croesus, and I would make sure that Crassus' wealth would be nothing by comparison with mine.[57]

LEGATE: All things are not given to everyone.[58]

BRUNO: So I see.

HENNO: What a wretch I am. I wish I had my two capons here and hadn't lost them. I can see I'm born under an unlucky star.

LEGATE: What's this about the capons Henno had?

BRUNO: He had them yesterday, but he gave them to the worthy Bartolinus for his advice.

LEGATE: That was not well done. He should have brought them here. Well, what can he pay? I'll let it go at that.

BRUNO: He can't pay you money, but he has two cows, which provide him with milk, butter, and cheese. He could sell one and keep the other to support his family. He would be taking the food out of his own mouth,[59] but he could bring the one here and sell it. He can't sell both cows, as you yourself will understand, or he would starve to death.

LEGATE: I wish he were rich. Wait here for me until I return. I'll consult with my people about what to do. I'll be back with you in a minute. [Exit Legate.]

BRUNO: Take courage, Henno. It's better to lose a cow than a son.

HENNO: If he'll accept the cow.

BRUNO: You bet he won't send you back empty-handed as long as you give him something, however little. And, Henno, I'm glad that I thought of advising you to make a vow to God before you entered the house, for he will be at your side now and help you.

HENNO: I am rightly fond of you, Bruno, and don't think that I'll forget your kindness.

[The Legate returns.]

LEGATE: [aside] My people said not to let him go, even if he pays me practically nothing. It isn't in my interest, first of all, so that I won't have to do without and secondly because I think that these people should get a notion of my liberality and benevolence. [To Henno] Now, Henno, since you can't give me anything more than a cow, you must make up for your poverty with industry and render me a service.

HENNO: If I can, I'll do it gladly. And what I can't do, my son will.

LEGATE: You can do it. Just advertise the great powers that have been given to me by the Apostolic See among your people at home, that is, among those who you know need such powers.

HENNO: I don't know your powers, but if you explain to me whatever powers you have, I'll make it my business to spread the news among my people to make sure that the shortfall you experience in my case will be made up abundantly from another source.

LEGATE: I'll explain, then.

BRUNO: And I'll do as my master told me to do and I myself want to do, and I'm sure I'll go away from here wiser.

LEGATE: You do well, especially if Henno here can't remember everything. First of all, then, it is agreed on the basis of Christ's gospel and the Acts of the Apostles, that the apostles themselves and Peter, foremost among the apostles, were sent to all regions of the world with powers given to them by Christ, to loose and bind everything on earth and to work more and greater miracles than Christ himself.[60] Their mission was through baptism to lead all nations to Christ, away from paganism and the cult of demons, and thus to make the whole world their domain. But when the apostles suffered death in various forms and departed for heaven, it is agreed that the Roman pope, Christ's supreme vicar, the head of the church and Peter's successor, was made Supreme Pontiff over all nations and all bishops whom the apostles had left behind as their successors and disciples. And since the city of Rome was the seat of government over all countries and nations, it was fair and square that it should also be the domicile of the head of the Christian religion, the one man who could bind and loose everything throughout the world, give and receive, institute and abrogate, send out and recall, order and prohibit, save and condemn. The remaining Christian nations and bishops were all under his power. This man had as much power in the whole world as others had over the churches in their own domain. By the verdict of this one man Roman kings and emperors would be chosen, and in accordance with this one man's will they would be rejected; no bishop could be appointed without his authorization; he alone held the scepter that ruled over kingdoms, nations, peoples, and cities. He alone governed war, peace, and treaties; in sum, one man was to receive everything and give everything.

This man, the head of the universal church, sent me as his universal representative to Germany, Denmark, and Sweden, just as Christ sent out his apostles. My mission was first to pour the treasure of Christ and of the church, that is, indulgences, into their lap and collect funds for the construction of a great church that is being built in Rome for St. Peter and to request on their behalf other things, which I'll list in a moment.

BRUNO [aside]: No one can deny the great power of the pope over the other bishops of the Christian commonwealth and extending

[handwritten marginal note: How the power pope has come into such power.]

to the Roman emperor, for even if it was not a fact that he was superior to them on account of his priestly honor, he was given that second sword bestowed on him a long time ago by the bishops of the Roman church. As for everything's being in the hands of one man, I leave that to men of greater learning whose proper business it is [to investigate such things]. All I know is that the mission on which Christ sent the apostles was very different from that on which the present pope sends his men. They were sent to preach evangelical law to the gentiles and unbelievers, to fish for men,[61] and to build living churches to the Holy Spirit, and to do so in abject poverty and in the face of imminent danger and death. As for you, we see you are sent to German believers, not so much to keep them loyal (for they are firm in their devotion), as to rob them of money, to fight not for souls but for the German treasure. The whole world will attest to the fact that this is your main objective. You are a new breed of apostle. You do not build living churches[62] to the Holy Spirit but churches of lifeless stone, and not in abject poverty or mortal danger but in wealth and pomp and luxury and wantonness. In fact, I hear that the last thing on their mind in Rome is building a church to Peter, and if they weave a cloth for show and to deceive the Germans, they completely undo it again at night[63] in the house of some cardinal. As if we were not burdened enough at home with the building of stone churches (although these churches we can enjoy at least, both in their magnificence and as works of piety).[64] I know, however, that there are among the Germans men with sharper eyes who, if you visited them, would perhaps let you taste the danger of death and let you experience what the apostles once suffered among the gentiles. In fact this came to pass recently in your dealings with the Danish king. But you suffered, not on account of your holiness, but because the Danes saw that you and your people resembled not the apostles of Christ but rather the apostles of Antichrist who they say will be sent from Babylon to sell everything, sacred or profane, for money, which is then to be used for every kind of debauchery by the Florentines and Romans, who laugh at the stupid Germans who let themselves be deceived.

LEGATE: What are you muttering there?

BRUNO: I am quietly pondering your sacred mission and comparing you with the apostles of Christ.

LEGATE: How can you compare us? The church today is very different from the church in former times.

BRUNO: My thoughts exactly. I was wondering how it could be that the church of Christ has changed, when I hear every day that Christ is living and that he is the solid foundation and the head of the church. And I am wondering likewise about the gospel which is to remain unaltered, even after heaven and earth are gone. Indeed I believe everything will take a turn for the better, and Christian charity and piety will be stronger and more perfect in men and women if we adjust our lives to the teaching of the gospel rather than resisting it and twisting Scripture to suit our desires—unless you preach to me a church of evildoers or Scribes and Pharisees,[65] of buyers and sellers (which is hateful to the Holy Spirit according to the prophet) whose tables Christ overturned and whom he threw out of his temple.[66] A church that disregards God's commands and establishes its own laws and claims to be Christian is lying, for it is a church whose head is not Christ himself but Satan, and the flames of fire will consume it.

LEGATE: It is blasphemy and heresy to say that the church whose head we hold to be the Supreme Pontiff is not the church of Christ. The gospel has not been changed one iota. We read and proclaim it ourselves every day. But to adjust our lives to it has always been difficult and is given only to perfect people and only to a very few who lived closer to the apostles' time. Do you see anyone today who is so perfect that he will hand over his shirt and coat to the man who wants to go to court for it or, when he is struck, turns the other cheek? Do you see anyone who loves his enemies, prays for his persecutors, and treats well those who hate him? In sum, anyone who loves his Lord with his whole heart and soul and nothing besides him, and loves his neighbor as himself? No, on the contrary, we return violence for violence, and if anything is seized from us unjustly, we go to court and fight for it, and we pay in the same coin that men paid us, and if we don't hate our enemies, we certainly don't love them or seek their company; we do care about God himself, but besides him, we care about business risks and collecting money and taking counsel for worldly things; and if we read our bible correctly, even the imperfect need not completely despair.

BRUNO: This may apply to the common people, but I know that the Lord disdains the lukewarm and wants us to be fervent in our belief. As far as I can see, the fact that our Christian devotion has grown cold is the responsibility of those who occupy Moses' seat and the place of the apostles. For the rest of the people measure their lives by their standard. If there were a spark of light left in them, the whole Christian realm would not be plunged into such complete darkness.

LEGATE: Enough of this. Make sure you understand this, Henno: I am the universal representative of the universally Supreme Pontiff who can do everything, and I am in charge of Germany.

HENNO: I understand.

BRUNO [aside]: I understand that he is the universal plague that infects everything by its touch.

LEGATE: Now listen to what else I can do by virtue of this power.

HENNO: I will.

BRUNO [aside]: No good—that's what you can do.

LEGATE: What?

BRUNO: Nothing. Go on, sir.

LEGATE: Now that the Christian faith has spread far and wide across the world, many churches have been established with priests and deacons. There is often disagreement among them, and to remedy any schism, one has been elected by the churches, who is in charge of the others, lest anyone pull Christ's church over into his corner and thus tear it apart. For this reason they created a superior rank occupied by the bishop, just as a general is appointed to command an army, or deacons elect the best among themselves and call him archdeacon. This was done everywhere, in Rome, in Gubbio, in Constantinople, in Reggio, in Alexandria, in Tanae: each man holds the position he merits and has the same authority to admonish, castigate, and punish his subjects. But if some people want to be under the authority of the bishop of their own choice, whether the case involves slander or any other accusation, I can interpose my authority in the name of the Supreme Pontiff who alone holds first place and has the greatest power, and they can obtain a judgment elsewhere from whomever they please. I even release them from the judgment passed on them by their own bishop and hand them over to judges who are convenient—do you understand, Henno?

HENNO: Not really. The parallel would be that I preside over a court case involving one of my people and you take away my authority to pass judgment on the slanderer or to inflict punishment on him, so that he can slander with impunity. Do you mean that?

LEGATE: That's my meaning exactly. You got it right. I deliver him from a lower to a higher court.

BRUNO: As far as I understand, it works like this. He is given money and creates a faction, acting no differently than if I kept sheep from obeying their shepherd or children from obeying their parents or students their teachers or citizens their officials or servants their masters. And as I see it, if we allow that to happen, what need is there for regional bishops whom we support at such cost, when the pope and his legates can prevent the bishops from settling the disputes in their own region and play bishops themselves, that is, want to be superintendents themselves? If they attempt to appoint judges over us at their pleasure, there will be no magistrates thereafter, no vicars of the bishop, no fiscals, no representatives of the German bishops—the priest will no longer obey his bishop, nor the deacon the priest. Everything will be upset and turned upside down and the last trace of church discipline will be lost. This was the message of the council of African bishops[67] to the pope who was demanding such tyrannical powers for himself. Many eyes, they said, saw more than one eye, individual judgments were more discerning than one overall judgment, the world was larger than a city, no one knew his flock better than the shepherd and could better feed, shear, and care for the flock when there was sickness or defend it against the wolf's attack.

LEGATE: I also have the power to reverse statements under oath made in contracts, wills, and all undertakings except those given to the papal court.

HENNO: I take it that you can also reverse pledges given by those captured by the enemy and sworn statements given to creditors that a debt will be paid at a given point in time, sacred pledges given to the fatherland, to the state, to kings, to holy houses, and to relatives?

LEGATE: Of course, and if there are any men who have entered the priesthood or a monastery and ceded a portion of their patrimony to their brothers in a contract under sign and seal and later renounce the contract, I restore their possessions to them and reverse the oath and refer it to the court. For I don't think it is fair that the clergy should be shortchanged of their property and laymen possess the goods that belong to the church.

BRUNO: "What does the dreadful thirst for gold not urge on men's hearts?"[68] . . . Open your eyes, Germans, it's plain to see for those who at last have recovered their senses: Deeds are done that have never been done before. Is this the mark of a papal legate, of a papal messenger, of an Angel of the light, or is this not rather the act of a criminal, a disturber of the peace, an evil genius aroused by every fury in his avarice? Awake and save your country!

LEGATE: What are you getting so excited about?

BRUNO: I cannot bear that Germany should lose its true faith and its ancient institutions because of your machinations. I wish I had never heard your words.

HENNO: Perhaps there are people who would want to put in a petition even for that and would find it useful—I'll tell them to come here.

BRUNO: No one would want it who is a good man and a Christian.

LEGATE: But there are some people who want it. I have also been given the power to create apostolic protonotaries and companions of the pope.

HENNO: What kind of men are those?

BRUNO: No doubt the bad eggs of a bad crow.[69]

LEGATE: They are the splendid men in black hats who are responsible to no bishop except to the Supreme Pontiff, who cannot be subjected to any court except that of the pope in Rome.

BRUNO: Have I not put my finger on it? They are the men who can commit many crimes with impunity, who can torment everyone with false accusations but are safe from prosecution themselves and cannot be touched because the pope has taken them under his wing. They are the men who obtain a great deal of money fraudulently and through false representations and then cheat their creditors, devising tricks suitable for their purposes.

LEGATE: I also confer doctorates.

BRUNO: Donkey doctorates.[70]

HENNO: I know for sure that our pastor wants one of those, for everyone thinks he is a learned man because he speaks nothing but Latin. I'll tell him and encourage him to come.

BRUNO: And will you confer wisdom and learning on the doctors too?

LEGATE: If they haven't got it already, I can't give it to them, but wisdom and learning are not bestowed on men even if they go to a regular university, for we see the greatest boors and fools honored with the red cap everywhere. If I had the power to confer the spirit of tongues, the spirit of knowledge and wisdom, wouldn't I charge a pretty penny for it?

BRUNO: I believe what you say. I recently met some men who returned from Rome with doctorates bestowed on them by the emperor in fact—men who have neither language skills nor knowledge nor wisdom, men who, it is said, can barely write, that is, are illiterate. Is that, too, part of the art of fishing for money—to honor fools?

LEGATE: I also create Counts Palatine and notaries.

BRUNO: God save me, and can you in your creativity also fashion creatures in your likeness, such as pallbearers and cardinals?

HENNO: What do you mean by "Count Palatine?" Is our prince-elector[71] dead together with his brothers? Anyone on whom you would bestow such a powerful principality would make you a god in return.

LEGATE: You don't understand. I only give them the insignia and arms and bestow on them nobility—it's up to them to make money with it somewhere. But if they have money, I give them permission to live in splendor. And if they have horses, permission to ride; if they don't have horses, they may walk.

HENNO: That's a privilege even I have been given. And can you really make others noble even though you are ignoble and mean yourself? I heard that nobility was once won through virtue and good deeds and courage in battle. Can it now be bought with money?

LEGATE: Such are the times.

HENNO: I know that much: there will be many who will want to buy nobility, even if they have to die of hunger, because it is such a heavy burden to be a countryman. This is an area in which you will make a great deal of money, sir. I just have one piece of advice, your Holiness: don't make any notaries.

LEGATE: And why not?

HENNO: If any come our way, we'll catch them, tie them up in a sack, and throw them into the water.

LEGATE: Even apostolic notaries?

HENNO: We make no distinction between public and apostolic notaries. They must die!

LEGATE: Who has introduced this punishment?

HENNO: The prince himself, for they are disturbers of peace and tranquillity and evil men.[72]

LEGATE: All of them?

HENNO: All the ones that ever came to us.

LEGATE: Furthermore, I absolve those who have been excommunicated because they assaulted priests and prelates of the church.

HENNO: How much do they have to pay?

LEGATE: Thirty ducats and up.

HENNO: A bargain! We have a priest in the neighborhood who has wronged many and sometimes even assaulted men when he was drunk, and he is insulting to everyone, sparing no one. But his victims don't dare to punish him in turn because he is sacrosanct. Yet no one's wife, no one's daughter, is safe from his wantonness. If they can kill him and be absolved from homicide for thirty ducats, they'll kill him immediately and you'll have your money.

LEGATE: I am not saying that they should kill him, but if they come to me, I'll absolve them. There will be mercy for the penitent.

BRUNO: Well spoken. Christ forbade them to touch his wounds;[73] this fellow counsels murder so that he can have his money. Not even bishops will be able to entertain the thought that they are sacrosanct; knives will be sharpened even against them, for a bishop is nothing but a priest, except for his rank. You have demonstrated that very well in Sweden, absolving with a nod both the tyrant's toady and the man who struck the archbishop. . . .

LEGATE: I'll even set aside the old law that no one must seek the kingly honor of priesthood before he is twenty-four years old.[74] If he comes to me at the age of twenty and asks to enter the sacred priesthood, I give him an apostolic letter to dispense with the law.

HENNO: That's easy to understand. It will come in handy for our children, for parents are very keen on seeing their sons made priests.

BRUNO: It is easy to see what money can do. How times have changed. How morals have changed. O splendid gold! It is a wonder that the Christian religion has not perished long ago, for I recently heard that in France a boy of barely fourteen years was made cardinal.[75] And this was not a case of transgressing a human law. Divine law was violated for the sake of money.

LEGATE: And if anyone should find the canonical hours[76] too heavy a burden, I'll give him permission to pray Roman style.

BRUNO: That's nice, praying Roman style is not to pray at all, yet I won't praise our people either who deafen God's ears with their laborious chanting of psalms. And they understand so little of it that they can't be sure whether they are praying or cursing. The teaching of the gospel is "Do not say long prayers as the pagans do."[77] And the Romans observe this point very well, and, so as not to err on the side of paganism, they say no prayers at all. This is such an established custom among them that a new Christian proverb has been coined: "praying like the Apostolic See," meaning of course, like something that does not and cannot pray since it is insensate.

LEGATE: If there are any priesthoods or benefices, as they call them, I have the authority to assign them for no less than four pure silver marks, or if someone wants to convert them or resign them for a pension, that can be done as well under my auspices.

HENNO: I don't understand a word.

BRUNO: I'm not surprised. I do understand it, though, because I know how all that buying and selling works. Simon is nothing by comparison; these men are the worst kind of Simons.[78] If you have money, you buy from the Romans whatever is for sale at the Fuggers[79] without any trouble. As for the more lucrative offices: the pontiff reserves those for sale by himself personally. For they yield what they call annates. And so that we might be left with nothing, like sheep that have become the prey of wolves, he sends men to sell the less profitable offices to us. And while all of this is going on we are carefree, sleeping like logs, as it were. If we wait any longer and let them go any further, they will sell the shirts off our backs to whomever they want, and throw our wives into the bargain. Has there ever been a worse idea than those so-called pensions? They are nothing but a pretext under which that notorious Simon is hiding, who holds first place in Christ's church as his vicar.

LEGATE: Do you remember all my powers, Henno?

HENNO: I'm trying hard.

LEGATE: Then let me see the fruit of your labor soon.

BRUNO: I'll be his fellow-canvasser, for I have learned an excellent lesson from you.

LEGATE: I have no use for your cow, Henno: sell it and bring me the money.

HENNO: It will be done.

LEGATE: In the meantime I'll write the document for you and have it sealed, and as soon as the money arrives, you'll find it ready and waiting for you.

HENNO: I'm off. Farewell, sir.

LEGATE: Farewell, both of you.

BRUNO: Go, Henno, and make haste.

HENNO: I will. Farewell meanwhile, my dear Bruno, you have done me a good turn.

BRUNO: Farewell.

NOTES

1. Translated from the Latin text in *Hutteni Opera omnia* (Leipzig, 1859–1870; repr. Aalen: Zeller, 1963), ed. E. Böcking, IV, 486–514. The full title is *Philalethis civis Utopiensis dialogus de facultatibus Rhomanensium nuper publicatus: Henno rusticus*, that is, *A recently published dialogue about the powers of the Romanists: Henno, a man from the country. By Philalethes, citizen of Utopia.* Philalethes means "Lover of the Truth."

2. On Hutten see p. 2.

3. For the Reuchlin affair see p. 2.

4. Polyphemus is the name of the man-eating giant in Homer's *Odyssey*; Polypragmon is no flattering name either. Its literal meaning is "doer of many things," but its (more common) metaphorical meaning is "busybody."

5. Public prosecutors and collectors of fines.

6. Literally, "I'll be reduced to work with a hoe," a quotation from Terence, *Heautontimorumenos* 5.1.58.

7. Cf. Terence, *Eunuchus* 5.3.4.

8. Aptly named after the author of a standard legal textbook, Bartolo da Sassoferrato (d. 1356). In the skit *The Robbers* (1521) Hutten called the legal profession "the school of Bartolists."

9. That is, blood-relationship. In church law, such a close relationship was an impediment to marriage, the usual remedy in such cases.

10. Indulgences were bought to release the soul of a deceased person from purgatory or to shorten its stay there. A contemporary jingle explains: "As soon as the coin in the coffer rings, the soul from purgatory springs." Luther's famous Ninety-Five Theses, posted in Wittenberg in 1517, protested the sale of indulgences and questioned their efficacy.

11. That is, the threat of excommunication. This description of the declining powers of Rome is reminiscent of Luther's letter to Pope Leo X (September 1520): "Today the name of the Roman Curia is a stench throughout the world, and papal

authority languishes. . . . what was once held in esteem is evil spoken of." For another echo see below, note 64.

12. Pope Leo X (d. 1521) was the second son of Lorenzo the Magnificent, ruler of Florence. He promoted other members of the Medici family to church offices and tried various schemes to establish his brother Giuliano in a principality. His conferring of the duchy of Urbino on his nephew Lorenzo led to an expensive war in 1517.

13. Thirty-one cardinals were created on June 26, 1517.

14. Virgil, *Aeneid* 3.216ff.

15. The reference is to Angelus Arcimboldus. Cf. L. Pastor, *History of the Popes*, 40 vols. (London: Kegan Paul, 1913–1932), VIII, pp. 450ff.

16. Italians, proud of their cultural pre-eminence in Europe, contemptuously referred to non-Italians as "barbarians." Needless to say, this chauvinism was greatly resented by other nations. See, for example, Irenicus' (Franz Gottlieb) *Exegesis Germaniae*, published in 1518: "[The Italians] attach the name 'barbarians' to us. Today the word should not be used at all except to describe the enemies of the Christian faith."

17. An expression used by Cicero, *Tusculan Disputations* 5.21.61.

18. Christian II (1481–1559). He came to the Danish throne in 1513 and reconquered Sweden in 1520, but his disastrous internal policies eventually led to his exile.

19. Antonelli Arcimboldus. He was finally released in 1523.

20. Perhaps an allusion to an expression in Juvenal, *Satires* 6.191: "They fornicate in Greek."

21. Matt. 6:6.

22. Sallust, *Jugurtha* 39. It was said of Pope Alexander VI that he "sells the keys, the altar, and Christ himself—and by rights, because he bought them for cash."

23. Matt. 10:8.

24. I.e., Bartolinus is suffering from a venereal disease.

25. Spoken in Italian; thus Henno's surprised reaction.

26. Bruno is reciting Vergil, *Aeneid* 2.65.

27. A line from a Roman comedy, Plautus, *Miles Gloriosus* 1.1.58.

28. Daily activities in a sixteenth-century household often began at daybreak.

29. Venus, Minerva, and Juno, who staged a beauty contest according to Greek mythology.

30. Paris, who was appointed judge by the goddesses, and who gave the prize to Venus because she promised him the most beautiful woman on earth: Helen of Troy. The further adventures of Paris and Helen led to the Trojan War.

31. Bruno uses a Latinized Greek phrase, *clini palaestrae.*

32. See above, note 15.

33. Payable on the installation of a new bishop.

34. In return for the right to nominate candidates the pope received "annates," the equivalent of one year's salary.

35. An ironic use of Rom. 2:11.

36. According to myth, Jupiter, struck by Ganymede's appearance, fell in love with him and had him carried off to Olympus where he made him his special attendant at meals. Jupiter's wife, Juno, was not amused.

37. The insignia of cardinals and papal protonotaries.

38. Proverbial; cf. H. Walther ed., *Lateinische Sprichwörter und Sentenzen des Mittelalters* (Göttingen: Vandenhoeck, 1966) No. 25637a.

39. Literally "Like lips, like lettuce," a proverbial expression; cf. Jerome, *Letters* 7.5.

40. *Testa de Buffalo*. He has not been identified.

41. Mythological figure with a hundred eyes.

42. Io had been turned into a heifer by her lover, Jupiter, to conceal her from his wife, Juno. When Juno discovered the deception, she set Argus to watch over her (cf. Hyginus, *Fables* 145).

43. The god Apollo is the champion of the Muses, depicted in mythology as lovely young women inspiring the artist.

44. Böcking (*Hutteni Opera omnia* IV, p. 487, note 31) explains that these were the penalties set out in the statutes of the city of Bamberg, articles 223.3.4 and 198.3.4.

45. Cf. for example, Isocrates, *Ad Nicoclem* 31, Cicero, *Laws* 3.14.31, and in the sixteenth century, Erasmus, *Education of a Christian Prince* (CWE 27, p. 219): "The common people imitate nothing with more pleasure than what they see their prince do."

46. A quotation from Roman comedy, Terence's *Heautontimorumenus* 4.2.6.

47. Of Uppsala; he forced the rightful bishop, Gustav Troll, to resign. See above, p. 27.

48. Alluding to the envoy's name "Angelus," angel.

49. Acts 8:18. Simon of Samaria offered the apostles money if they would share their miraculous power with him.

50. That is, the Apostle Peter.

51. According to Livy 22.51.

52. That is, excommunication.

53. Terence, *Phormio* 4.4.5.

54. He is referring to the Apostle Paul's ambitious task to bring the gospel message to non-Jews.

55. Gen. 9:29.

56. However, the legate has cited only from the Old Testament.

57. Croesus, king of Lydia, and Crassus, with Caesar a member of the triumvirate, were proverbial for their wealth.

58. A quotation from Vergil, *Eclogues* 8.63.

59. A quotation from Terence, *Phormio* 1.1.9.

60. Cf. Matt. 16:19.

61. Cf. Matt. 4:19.

62. Cf. 1 Peter 2:5.

63. An allusion to Penelope, heroine of Homer's *Odyssey*, who had promised to choose a husband after completing her work on the loom. To put off the decision, she secretly undid at night the work she had done during the day.

64. The passage is reminiscent of Luther's words in the *95 Theses:* "First of all we should raise up living temples, not local churches, and last of all St. Peter's which is not necessary for us. We Germans cannot attend St. Peter's."

65. Ps. 25:5.

66. Matt. 21:12.

67. A reference to the conflict between Pope Stephen II (d. 257) and the African bishops, among whom Cyprian was most vocal.

68. Virgil, *Aeneid* 3.56.

69. Proverbial, cf. Zenobius 4.82.

70. Literally, "troubles, not doctorates"; the pun *dolores/doctores* cannot be rendered into English.

71. Ludwig V (d. 1544), whose title was "Elector Palatine." Henno confuses "Elector Palatine" with "Count Palatine," an honorific title.

72. The legal profession was unpopular; perhaps this is an allusion to Thomas More's *Utopia*, in which the practice of law was forbidden. Cf. also the popular verse (Hans von Westernach, *Ein Straflied*, ca. 1470):

> A profession's gained the upper hand
> And caused much uproar in the land;
> I speak of jurists and doctors of law—
> A more harmful lot you never saw.

73. John 20:17.

74. Cf. Gratian's *Decretals* I. chs. 5–7, dist. 77.

75. Jean, son of René, Duke of Lotharingen, in 1518.

76. Obligatory prayers for clerics.

77. Matt. 6:6.

78. See above, note 49.

79. A prominent banking firm in Augsburg that was known to finance such transactions; see also below, page 70, note 45.

2

A Reuchlinist's Ascent to Heaven

THE AUTHOR, Ortvinus Gratius (d. 1542), was the descendant of an impoverished Dutch noble family. Like his contemporary Desiderius Erasmus, he attended Latin school in Deventer. In 1501 he matriculated at the University of Cologne where he obtained a B.A. (1502) and an M.A. (1506). In 1507 he began teaching in the faculty of arts. A few years later he took holy orders. When he became involved in the Reuchlin affair, it was on Hoogstraten's side (see p. 2). As a result, he soon found himself the butt of humanistic satire. Many of the fictitious *Letters of Obscure Men* were addressed to him. In reply, Gratius published *Lamentations of Obscure Men* (Cologne, 1518), but his effort to match wits with his opponents was a mixed success. Although the book has some amusing passages, Gratius' humor is, on the whole, heavy-handed. The following dialogue,[1] which comes from the *Lamentations*, is one of the more skillfully executed passages. It lampoons the preoccupation of the humanists with classical antiquity, pokes fun at their custom of quoting classical authors at every step, and parodies their use of extravagant poetical language and outlandish terms that only a specialist could understand. Gratius also depicts the humanists as semi-pagans, who would rather invoke the help of Apollo and the Muses than the Catholic saints and who speak of the classical gods in terms that Christians traditionally reserved for Jesus. The dialogue is significant because it links classical learning with unorthodox thought, a tendency that led by degrees to the identification of humanism with the Reformation. Erasmus early on recognized the danger of such generalizations. Sounding the alarm, he wrote about Gratius' *Lamentations*: "I am surprised that theologians and professed followers of a religious life should stir up trouble of this kind, the outcome of which must be quite uncertain."[2] A few years later he noted that his fears had been realized. Luther had become the center of controversy, the church was heading toward schism, and the humanities were suffering by association. Monks and theologians, he wrote, had cunningly managed "to link the cause of the Muses with that of Luther."[3] Erasmus was disappointed that Gratius had joined the camp of anti-Reuchlinists:

> What came into Gratius' head, that he should be willing to prostitute his literary skill, such as it is, to the folly, or more truly the ambition, of certain individuals, when he seems endowed with gifts which, coupled with serious work and sound judgment, might have given him a place among the stylists and men of letters? As it is, the only feat he is known for is his abuse of Reuchlin and his friends, and his having apparently lent the aid of a hack scribbler, writing for his bread, to spiteful men who cannot write.[4]

A DIALOGUE BETWEEN MERCURY AND POTLICKER

Jupiter recently called a council of all the gods and announced that he wanted a prudent and learned man to substitute for him in heaven. He complained that he was quite undone by old age and could no longer govern the course of the planets and manage the whole machinery of heaven. He was therefore looking for a learned and wise man, as I said, to be the curator of antiquities and diligent guardian of the celestial gate, to light up the moon when its fire had gone out, and to guard vigilantly against any of the gods disturbing Jupiter when he was sleeping with his sister Juno;[5] also to see to it that the horses of the sun[6] not go astray and plunge into the ocean or be overcome by the noonday heat. "And to this man," said Jupiter, "I shall give the task of turning obscure men into evil demons and placing them with their created souls on their companion stars.[7] For he will have the task to see to it that the planet Saturn does not conflict with the celestial sign of the Virgin, and he will be in charge of many other things. And he will be considered worthy of my majesty and the hospitality of the gods."

Jupiter's command was very surprising and quite unheard-of. When all the gods had nodded in agreement, Mercury, the messenger of the immortal gods, who excels the others by far in eloquence, was sent to this humble abode of the living, which we call the earth. When he had searched almost the whole globe on the initiative of the gods (for they did not want a man to be appointed to an office which was proper to themselves), he chose out of the whole number of obscure men a Reuchlinist, indeed very much a Reuchlinist, who had never had a liking for the theologians. This man's name was Potlicker Reuchlin-friend. . . . Mark the deep mystery, illustrious gentlemen.[8] Here was a man of learning, able to understand celestial matters, although he had no respect for universities and had never studied in any faculty of letters. For if I judge the man rightly (and I know him), we shall find in him neither a philosopher, nor a theologian, nor a jurist, nor a physician, nor a man of letters. Now, Mercury, who can imitate and disguise anything and was sent on this impossible mission on the initiative of the gods, appeared with a blaze of light to this obscure Reuchlinist, whose name was Potlicker, as he was sleeping. Having no experience with celestial matters, he was terribly afraid, when he saw Mercury. "His hair bristled" (as Virgil says in Book III)[9] and his voice stuck in his throat. But Mercury had brought from the heavens above some sweets and offered him ninety-nine of what is commonly called "Basensche Koechen."[10]

MERCURY: Eat, dear Potlicker, and grow stout. For a long journey awaits you.

POTLICKER (thinking that Mercury was an angel and he himself another sun): Where are we going?

MERCURY: To heaven.

POTLICKER: Then it's right that I should nourish my soul there and my body here. Now I sense Jupiter's kindness. . . . Your god did well, and not without reason he recognized me as his friend and the prince of all Reuchlinists. Well done, I say. Your celestial food was so pleasant, I no longer feel sick. But I cannot converse with you, Mercury, because I am quite exhausted on account of my past illnesses and miseries.

MERCURY: Have you too suffered misery among the gluttons and sycophants?

POTLICKER: How can you, the gods' messenger, be ignorant of this? How can you foretell the future if you don't know the past? If I had conversed with the gods all these days, I would be a god like you and the others.

MERCURY: Watch your words. For it is written: "Nothing in excess." Did not Hesiod sing to the lyre "The tongue is man's greatest treasure and a great gift is a sparing tongue when it keeps measure"?[11]

POTLICKER: Beautiful verses!

MERCURY: Right—so stop raving. Do not measure everyone by your own standards and stop your sickening insolence. Do not harass others with your impudent words. They are not going to make you friends in heaven. Or are you looking for enemies?— Well, let us not quarrel, just tell me in a word where you got that grave and clearly bothersome illness?

POTLICKER: From eating many and varied foods.

MERCURY: What food do you commonly eat?

POTLICKER: Skin of goose, roast capon necks, veal from a young heifer, turtle doves, partridge, pheasant, quail, thrush, figpeckers, and other delicacies of this kind, carefully cooked tender. But they no longer harm my stomach because it is now like an empty slate which has nothing written on it that is "fit or able" to be depicted,[12] and I am always mindful of the line "He who ingests, digests, and egests well is in good health."

MERCURY: Right you are. You'll live a long life among us if you are so respectful of your stomach.

POTLICKER: How long will I live?

MERCURY: For ever and ever.

POTLICKER: O lucky me, O blessed Potlicker! And while we are on the subject of dinner, tell me, please, before we leave here, what food do the immortal gods eat? For I am a gourmet, an eager attendant at table everywhere in the city.

MERCURY: We eat ambrosia, suck eggs, have sugar candy and fat cows' udders and pastry flavored with almonds and sugar. Sometimes we have whole roast pig. We allow only him to approach to our table who has adjusted his belt according to the famous verse "When you intend to sup, your belt needs loosening up." And in the same vein, "When food your stomach does encumber, then you will likely want to slumber."

POTLICKER: What do I hear, holy Juno, what do I hear? Take me there quickly, holy Mercury, take me there.

MERCURY: Let us go then, for we must hurry.

POTLICKER: First I need to find some jugs of wine.

MERCURY: Hurry up.

POTLICKER: Go ahead, I'll follow. [As they departed, some obscure men cried: "Holy Father, remember us when thou comest into thy kingdom!"[13]]—You beasts! Only I am worthy of such honor.

In short, the two marched on, and when they came to Mount Parnassus,[14] Potlicker could not lift himself up to heaven from there.

So they put Etna on Parnassus and Olympus on Etna and placed many mountains on top of each other. That done, Mercury said:

MERCURY: Let's ascend the mountains.

POTLICKER: Pull me up behind you.

MERCURY: That's a difficult task.

POTLICKER: How so?

MERCURY: Because you are now big, fat, and bloated.

POTLICKER: Let me move my bowels, so I'll be lighter.

MERCURY: As you please, but don't be too long about the business. (While Potlicker was ducking into a corner, Mercury said:) I wish that Reuchlinist ass (he isn't worthy of the name) would move his lungs and liver with his bowels. What a fetid smell. What a stinking old goat! Reuchlin would have been well served if this man had never been born. (So saying, he shouted:) Where is that man Potlicker?

POTLICKER: Stuck on the rock.

MERCURY: I wish you were stuck there forever. Come on, slow-poke, fat lump!

POTLICKER: Look, here I am, faster than a cart, more "fleeting than a deer."[15] I don't need your help now.

MERCURY: We'll see. I'm going ahead.

POTLICKER: Look, I'm on top of Olympus. I've caught up with you. I'm "sailing safely in the harbor"[16] and gazing upon heaven's stars.

MERCURY: You've done all right.

POTLICKER: One more leap and I'm in heaven.

MERCURY: We'll see. Just watch that you don't destroy Plato's Ideas.[17]

POTLICKER: Who are these beastly things?

MERCURY: What you call "beastly things" are the former priest-
esses of Apollo. They are indeed toothless old women. After they
cast off their bodies, they were placed among the stars, like images
of things.[18]

POTLICKER: By God, what do I hear from you? I've read twenty-
five books of Aristotle's *Ethics*[19] but I couldn't understand anything he said about the Ideas.

MERCURY: It's no surprise you couldn't understand it. You are no
philosopher, you are just a plain little grammarian. But jump up
into heaven quickly.

POTLICKER: I'm steeling myself for the task. Don't touch me.

MERCURY: I won't. But careful that you don't fall.

As that bold Potlicker stretched up high toward heaven and raised
his insolent head while jumping, he fell down from Olympus onto
Etna and from there into the cesspool of Vulcan, who used to live
there in the olden times.[20] Then Mercury laughed loudly and exclaimed repeatedly: "O Corydon, O Corydon, what madness has
taken hold of you? White blossoms fall and dark hyacinths are
gathered!"[21]

POTLICKER: O holy Mercury, help me! O Apollo, O Latona, and
you, O nine Muses, help me!

Moved by these lamentations, Mercury picked up the blinded
man, now stinking like the plague, and brought him to some new
horse-fountain,[22] just discovered by the Spirit of the Woods. There
he wanted to cleanse the man, but by mistake he drowned him.
The result is that even today the water of that fountain is turbid
and smelly, and whoever is ill-advised enough to drink from it,
will become insane rather than wise.

NOTES

1. Text translated from the Latin in *Lamentationes obscurorum virorum* (Cologne, 1518) bii[r-v] (in *Hutteni Opera omnia*, Suppl. I, pp. 351–55).

2. *Ep.* 830:4–6 (CWE).

3. Cf. *Epp.* 1716:34–37 (1526), 1805:49–63 (1527) (Allen).

4. *Ep.* 856:22–28 (CWE).

5. In ancient mythology Jupiter, the king of the gods, was married to his sister, Juno.

6. In Greek and Roman mythology the sun god traveled the sky in a chariot drawn by four horses.

7. According to Plato's myth of creation, there were "souls equal in number to the stars" and each soul was assigned a specific star (*Timaeus* 41).

8. *Viri illustres*, a clear reference to the title of Reuchlin's collection of letters, *Epistolae illustrium virorum*. See p. 2.

9. Virgil, *Aeneid* 3.48.

10. Perhaps "Aunt's cookies," from German *Base*, "aunt."

11. Hesiod, *Works and Days* 694, 707–708.

12. Cicero, *Orator* 1.22.99.

13. In the Bible these words are addressed to Jesus (Luke 23:42).

14. Mountain sacred to Apollo and the Muses.

15. Virgil, *Georgics* 3.539.

16. Terence, *Andria* 3.1.22.

17. According to Plato's epistemology, the form of a thing, akin to an abstract concept, but having a real existence outside of our senses.

18. According to Plato's creation myth, "he who lived well during his appointed time was to return and dwell in his native star" (*Timaeus* 42).

19. Potlicker is exaggerating. The Aristotelian work contains only ten books. Aristotle comments on Plato's Ideas in *Ethics* 1095–1097.

20. Vulcan is the god of fire.

21. Virgil, *Eclogues* 1.18, 69. The eclogue is the lament of a spurned lover.

22. *Fontem caballinum*, literal translation of Greek "Hippocrene," a fountain sacred to the Muses. The Latin comes from the Roman satirical poet Persius, *Prol.* 1, who also uses it sarcastically.

3

Theologists in Council

JOHANNES JÄGER (1480–ca. 1545) was the son of a Thuringian peasant. He became a priest and studied at Cologne and Erfurt, where he graduated with a Master's degree in 1507. After the fashion of his age, he Latinized his name, calling himself Crotus Rubianus, that is, Ruby (or Ruddy) Hunter.[1] He was a friend of Ulrich von Hutten, a strong supporter of Johann Reuchlin,[2] and during the early 1520s sympathetic toward Luther. Between 1517 and 1520 he lived in Italy and obtained a doctorate of theology from the prestigious University of Bologna. On his return he taught at the University of Erfurt. After a stint in the service of the duke of Prussia, he was appointed councilor to Albert of Brandenburg, archbishop of Mainz. By that time he had turned away from Luther, publicly criticizing him in an *Apologia* (1531). A master of satire, Jäger was one of the principal authors of the *Letters of Obscure Men*.[3] The following dialogue, which is set in 1520, belongs to the Lutheran phase in his life. Once falsely attributed to Hutten, the piece was first published in a collection of skits entitled *Seven Witty and Candid Dialogues*, which appeared without date or place under the pseudonym "Corallus," that is, "Coral," which may be construed as a synonym of Rubianus, "Ruby."[4] The dialogue remained popular for two centuries and was reprinted on its own as well as in conjunction with the *Letters of Obscure Men*, for the last time in 1757.

In *Theologists in Council*[5] Jäger presents the fictitious minutes of a faculty meeting called to plan an effective strategy against reformers and humanists. The meeting is chaired by Jacob Hoogstraten, the Dominican inquisitor and principal foe of Reuchlin.[6] Among those assembled are prominent theologians from Cologne and Louvain, the two universities that first condemned Luther. The speakers do not discuss the doctrinal positions of the reformers but their methodology, expressing dismay at Luther's rejection of scholastic authorities in favor of Scriptural prooftexts and at the humanists' insistence on a knowledge of the three biblical languages. Among the actions advocated by various speakers are: banning the books of these new "heretics"; lobbying the emperor to take action against them; persuading the pope to bribe Luther with a lucrative church office; and staging an epiphany in support of their own position. Farfetched as the last two suggestions may appear, they had in fact close parallels in history. In 1509 three Dominicans claimed that the Virgin had appeared to them endorsing their position on the immaculate conception; their claims were exposed as fabrications and they were put to death.[7] There is no evidence of plans in Rome to placate Luther with promotions, but there were allegations that another influential writer, Desiderius Erasmus,[8] had been bribed in this fashion. Champions of the reform, disappointed with Erasmus' policy of restraint, interpreted the generosity of his patrons and the conciliatory attitude toward him in Rome as a ploy to draw him into the Catholic camp. There were rumors that Pope Paul III was about to make Erasmus a cardinal, but the latter declared that he would not accept the appointment and vigorously denied that his views had been influenced by favors shown him in the past.

  Jäger's skill in parodying the theologians' leaden style and the jargon of official documents contributes greatly to the effectiveness of his lampoon.

A meeting of theologists[9] to deal with the champions of Germany and of good literature, held on April 16, after Jacob Hoogstraten was relieved of his duties as prior and inquisitor.[10]

HOOGSTRATEN, acting dean of the faculty of theology: Since, as the apostle says,[11] "there must be heresies so that good men will be made manifest," esteemed gentlemen and professors, I, Jacob Hoogstraten, acting dean of the faculty of theology at the University of Cologne, in fulfillment of my oath, had Your Professorships called together for a consultation concerning such teachings as are heretical, scandalous, blasphemous, and offensive to pious ears, and to hear your opinion, gentlemen. For although in the year past we condemned, by due process, the propositions of a certain brother from the order of St. Augustine[12] on account of their being completely worthless, yet because said brother does not cease to lead the people astray with his corrupt teaching, calling us heretics, Pharisees, and boors ignorant of Scripture, I thought it necessary to sift once more through those same propositions as well as through numerous dialogues by other writers, that we may burn the chaff with inextinguishable fire.[13] Nevertheless, as is the custom, before I proceed to the vote, I wish first to hear the opinions of the professors. Let the beadle be called in and diligently note down everything.

HOOGSTRATEN: Professor Duplex,[14] as I said, what is your opinion about those new poets and those novelties which are produced now by that devilish art of printing—if we leave them alone, everyone will take their side and be converted to the new fashion and disdain the holy theology of the Holy Doctor[15] and our other predecessors; and those pseudoscholars will come and take away our kingdom and we shall no longer be able to impose on or deceive old women and corrupt princes with our evil counsels when we hear their confession; and consequently, when we preach before the people against those scoundrels and slander them, the peasants will not believe us; and consequently, they will not give us cheese and eggs and ham when we go to the country.[16] Therefore I say: Better to take thought than to be taken in.

DUPLICIUS: Excellent and exceedingly learned Professor Hoogstraten, I don't know what to say. I dearly wish I had said this long before. But as the poet says: "The sowherds come late."[17] Now it's going to be a lengthy business and complex beyond calculation. I know no better way than to leave them to their follies. That is the best way. For if we resist, they won't care about our phrasicalities, and we'll upset the people. And even if they recommend it a hundred times, I won't learn Greek and Hebrew![18] I can hardly read the Psalter—and now they want me to read these fantasies. It's a waste of time. But for the sake of peace, it is my opinion, as I said, that we should leave them alone, or else they will write against us and make us notorious for ever and ever.[19]

HOOGSTRATEN: You are partly right, Professor, but it seems to me that you are called Duplicius because you are of two minds and inclined toward the opponents' side, and therefore you are most suspect to me when you say that we should leave them alone. Didn't I explain before that they will corrupt the whole world if we leave them alone? And then the Holy Doctor and Capreoli and Durandus and Herveus[20] and the other pillars of the church will be thrown under the bench into the dust. Therefore I call on Professor Edward Lee[21]—you are braver and you have an old grudge against Erasmus and Martin Luther and their followers. You are, moreover, a good Scotist and have the zeal of your Subtle Doctor[22]—what then is your opinion?

LEE: With your leave, Professor, may I speak a word?

HOOGSTRATEN: Even a hundred, if you please.

LEE: I never approved of that new fashion and those new doctors,[23] Jerome, Augustine, Athanasius, and those poets,[24] even though I don't know what they wrote and can't understand it; yet so that I may be said to have truly lived among men and have made for myself a name among the great names, I have wasted three years in which, to console myself when I wasn't reading Scotus, I often read Greek after breakfast and scanned those Greek doctors—just as our bachelors read the *Sentences*.[25] But, holy God, what can I say, I found nothing but lies in them, I found that Erasmus had falsified the New Testament,[26] that this isn't at all what's in our version[27]—that genuine version of Jerome as he controverted it himself.[28] Nevertheless I admonished the man charitably to mend his ways and, if he had any sense, add my annotations to his. Thereupon he showed such arrogance that he used my notes to wipe his behind.[29]

HOOGSTRATEN: I had a good inkling that the two of you weren't on good terms. The snake is hiding in the grass![30] It is amazing how much contempt he has shown for you, and yet they say he is very friendly and speaks and writes even for children. But go on.

LEE: Perhaps he does, but I hate him nevertheless with my whole heart, for he isn't a good Scotist, and I have written a book against him.[31] I think you have already seen it. And I shall write a great deal more against him because I feel that I am making progress in Greek and I want to study Greek still further so that I may traduce him before the bishops, the pope, and the cardinals; and I shall take special care to plot against him before the Derthusian,[32] the enemy of all students.

HOOGSTRATEN: Be bold and don't worry. I can see that he doesn't worry about you.

LEE: I'll do it, I will. And I won't have any scruples about it, and although I have anger in my heart I can still say Mass every day, for it is hatred for a cause not a person, as the Holy Doctor says, Book II, chapter 2, article 1e, paragraph 3, fig. i in his solution to the first argument, at the end of line 4. I do not feel hatred for the person, because I do not hate Erasmus, who is a creature of God, but I do hate good literature, as they call it, which he promotes. And he leads astray all young students with his translations.[33]

HOOGSTRATEN: Fair and square! I hate Johann Reuchlin the same way, although everyone says that he is a man of great integrity, and I hate Martin Luther, Peter of Ravenna,[34] and Hutten,[35] and many others, because envy moves me and I cannot see that they taught and wrote well.

LEE: In sum, here is my proposal: Let us draw up a new regulation with a privilege from the Pope and the Universities of Cologne and Louvain, that no one in the halls of our great university shall endeavor or presume to read, publicly or privately, the works of those new poets, on penalty of six gold marks and expulsion from the university. Furthermore, that the booksellers and printers shall not publish, print, sell, buy, or in any way convey these books to our colleges, on penalty of losing their citizenship if they are residents (or their life if they are foreigners), of forfeiting all their books, and of being imprisoned until they redeem themselves with those said six gold marks, which money is to go into the funds of the theological faculty so that whenever and wherever it may be necessary to call a meeting against the heretics, the faculty will have a good dinner from that money.

HOOGSTRATEN: That is a good proposal. That is what we should do. Next, Professor Eck,[36] I can see the ideas moving in your head.[37] Tell us what you have thought up against those poets.

ECK: What can I say? You are acting like the Pharisees[38] who came with the Herodians to question Christ about Caesar's coin and sent one to speak on behalf of all, thinking in their cunning, if he succeeded, they would all appear victorious, but if he did not succeed, no blame would attach to them. Just so you incited me against Luther. You sent me many letters because I am well versed in the *Parva Logicalia*[39] and in the compilations of Tinctor[40] of the professors in the Bursa Koeeck,[41] and in the other holy doctrines of the Doctors of the church, that is to say, of Scotorellus, Alexander of Hales, Landulphus, etc.[42] — but because I had no success, you covered me with muck, kept your distance, and left me stuck in the mud. What then should I advise you to do?

HOOGSTRATEN: No, Professor, that's not the case at all! We don't want you to be stuck in the mud. We have come together here to help you to confound and scatter all who wish us ill.

ECK: Nothing doing. You won't succeed. I believe I am as knowledgeable as you in the teachings of the Holy Doctor, yet I was unsuccessful because that man [Luther] denies everything and cannot be bothered with syllogisms. As soon as I produce a neat argument and have come up with a conclusion according to Frisemorum or Berbelin or Braca,[43] he throws out the conclusion and the whole argument and says that these are fantasies and snares laid by men who have no business with theology. And he wants us to cite the gospel or Paul or a text from Holy Writ instead of syllogisms. But where are we to get them? Our quivers are empty. I have taken great pains in my defense of the pope[44] over the pros and cons, so that he might give me a fat prebend or bishopric, and I wrote to professors everywhere, slandering and criticizing Luther, and yet I was defeated. Furthermore, all those who are now writing want to dissociate themselves from me and make me out a fool who has begun to build up something and cannot finish it. But I was bold and shameless and cared nothing for all of this; I screwed up my courage and acquired two synodal codicils through the intercession of the Fuggers,[45] and I journeyed to the sacred city that is a den of thieves,[46] that is, to Rome, and I kissed the feet of the pope in hopes of suppressing my enemy. When the pope saw this, he commended my great zeal very highly, but so far he hasn't rewarded me as I hoped he would. He merely called a meeting of cardinals to excommunicate Luther. But except for two, they wouldn't agree to it. One[47] was from the Medici family and had been promoted to the cardinalate through simony; the other[48] is a great flatterer of the pope. So when this didn't succeed, I plotted with several others and laid down much lint and kindling which in time might be fanned into a great fire.

But to the task at hand: since we are all congregated here for this purpose I will—you know me—stand tall[49] and serve, and I will in the end be victorious and celebrate a triumph over that heretic, and when he is at the stake, I want to light the fire in the woodstack. I want to be his executioner. You do likewise and defend your teaching. And if you so decide, we shall sway Charles,[50] the Catholic Monarch, with money and the intercession of that D.[51] whom he has at his court, for that man is a good theologist. Otherwise, I have no further advice. The pope is lying low; the secular professors are against us. You Dominicans and Carmelites have served bravely so far; so have the Carthusians, except for three or four who uphold this new fashion. We must have Charles on our side; if he rejects us (and I'm afraid that this will happen), it's all over.

HOOGSTRATEN: But for a long time the other side, too, has called on Charles, as in the recently published letter of Count Neuenahr.[52]

ECK: Then we must find a means of forestalling them. Ask others who are perhaps more experienced in stuff of this sort.

HOOGSTRATEN: Professor Arnold,[53] you have a singular gift for devising slander. You know what wonderful counsel you gave us with respect to Reuchlin. What are we to do in this case?

ARNOLD: None of you knows a thing. There you are wrapped up in your wonderful speculations, but you haven't learned how this world works. If every one of you were sent to the stake, you wouldn't come up with a single good idea to save yourselves. You reason because you have no experience. And you know nothing of this world, except perhaps as far as avarice and envy goes, because according to the proverb "Every theologist is S-upercilious, A-varicious, and L-ivid with envy" (and you may add "with a T-aste for luxury"), according to the etymology of the word SALT, as is written: "You are the SALT of the earth."[54]

HOOGSTRATEN: Holy God, Professor, you speak the truth! There are some among us who know how to dispute and spin subtle arguments, but when they come home from a morning's lectures and want to eat, the kitchen is still cold and the cook still asleep, or holed up in some monastery with some monk, where she has the audacity to—ahem!

ARNOLD: But this isn't about getting your dinner. You remember well how we proceeded when we wanted to prove that the Blessed Virgin was conceived in original sin, etc.?[55] Let's do the same thing in the present case. Unless we prove by a miracle that our theology is better than that of the poets, we lose our shirts, and our papers are worthless. Listen to my advice, then. I am a good necromancer and can transform an angel of darkness into an angel of light[56] and I can transform anyone I want. If you agree, I play the Holy Doctor, you can be Scotus, and Professor Balduinus can be St. Anthony, and each of us must carry a golden book in his hand. And in addition I'll put a dove above my head to represent the Holy Spirit. And at night we'll go to the bed of Brother Petrus, the Dominican lecturer. And I'll go first and whisper into his ear: "I am Thomas and I have written all I have written by the inspiration of the Spirit and I never erred in my writings and those who followed my teaching never strayed from the Roman Church." Then you do likewise. And afterward we'll suddenly fly through the window with a great flash lighting up the room. In the morning, when he rises, he will immediately preach about his vision to the people. And I have a spirit, with whom I am on familiar terms, whom I'll send to Luther's and Erasmus' bedside at night, that they may be troubled and vexed.

HOOGSTRATEN: That would be splendid, but there is the risk of our being betrayed and mixed up with what happened in Bern.[57] I don't want any part of this play. If you want to, go ahead and try, as long as you don't drag me into it. May your sins fall upon your own head. It is not a good thing to joke about the saints. Our order learned this to its detriment with those false miracles. But if you know of anything else, lawful or not, speak up boldly. I'll grant you absolution—even if someone confessed to me that he had killed Reuchlin, no one would find out and I would absolve him completely. So there.

ARNOLD: I have no other advice. Those laymen and students are getting wise and know how to watch out. They don't allow themselves to be deceived easily. I hand the matter over to you and the other faculty members.

HOOGSTRATEN: Next, Professor Petrus, you are a very zealous monk, you don't eat meat, and you keep your hands busy so that you won't have book learning in your community. What is your opinion, have you any plan to fight these scoundrels?

PETRUS: My dear professor, I have no plan. This whole world is corrupt and full of heretics. In my time, when I was your disciple, it was different. I am trying hard but making no headway. And so I agree with what Professor Duplicius said: leave them alone. Perhaps it is the will of heaven that a new era should begin every forty years. You will see, just as they now drag into the light Jerome and Chrysostom and those other poets, so after forty years the teaching of St. Thomas will be brand-new again and more admired than ever, because men are always looking for something new. It's not very well possible to burn all the books in the libraries. So take courage and leave them alone. When they have had their fill and are sick of the business, they'll stop.

HOOGSTRATEN: Next, Professor Scropha,[58] is that your opinion also?

SCROPHA: Not at all. If we allow the gospel to come to light, all the old heresies—Arianism, Manichaeism, Helvidianism, and the others—will return. Don't you know that, when those old Doctors reigned, there were many heresies in the church of God, which now by the grace of God are all extinct and brought to ruin through the most holy doctrine of the Holy Doctor and of the Subtle Doctor, Scotus? And if they hadn't appeared on the scene, I don't know where we would be. So if you put up with them, you most definitely aren't good Christians and lack zeal for the house of God.

HOOGSTRATEN: I would gladly do what I can, but you see the diversity of opinions among our professors. Next, Professor Lupold.

LUPOLD[59]: "Do not transgress the limits set by your father," says the Wise Man.[60] We have received this teaching from our teachers before us. Why would we want to abandon their heavenly doctrine? If you want to reject scholastic theology and logic and metaphysic, who will dispute against the heretics? Who will convert the Jews and gentiles to the faith? How are we to preach before the people and resolve cases of conscience? Who will defend the pope and the traditions of man, if we are willing to accept their fantasies? To perdition with their ribald stories. I would rather go to the stake than study those new things.

HOOGSTRATEN: By the devil, I wouldn't. I want to fight for the Holy Doctor unto death by fire, but exclusively not inclusively. Ha, ha ha. As you know, they themselves do not completely reject logic and philosophy, but say that we don't have the true skill and have so far taught nothing but stuff and nonsense and cavils which are not found in Aristotle. And they spit on the venerable Peter of Spanheym and Tartaretus and the *Copulata*[61] and the Eckian dreams. There has now arisen a man by name of Philip Melanchthon,[62] of whom they have great hopes. He has devised a new logic and a new rhetoric and said that rhetoric is half logic and that one depends on the other and they share the basic principles. I don't understand a word of it.

LUPOLD: My dear man, don't believe them. Who would want to teach those donkeys? They want to correct the *Copulata* and Bricot and Tartaretus[63]—a fine thing, by God! They want to be Greeks, but if they came to the Holy Land and had to beg for bread in the name of God in Greek or Hebrew, they would know nothing— and they want to correct our translation, as if the Holy Doctor, who was without doubt truly holy, had not understood Aristotle.

HOOGSTRATEN: I certainly wish you spoke the truth, Professor, but unfortunately they are taught by native speakers of Hebrew and Greek, who are certainly able and willing to teach them the idioms of their language. You are angry and upset. Next, Professor Stentor,[64] you too are unlutheran,[65] as you have shown in your sermons and loud declamations before the people, saying that they must not believe the words of Luther or read his books. If only all graduates would act like you, but nowadays there is a lack of zeal and no concern for the traditions of the ancients and the elders. Thus, dear professor, what is to be done to oppress that heretic?

STENTOR: Venerable and excellent Professors, it is true, I sometimes preach against those writers of new things because they are heretics, but I can see that I am making no headway. They allow us to rant and rave, but they go on sowing their tares. They don't care about our curses, and thus it is written of the sons of Israel in Egypt, the more they are oppressed by the Pharaoh and thrown into the dust, the more they will flourish.[66] And so they let us sing our song and go on doing what they do, and we make no progress; rather we are confounded ourselves. Let me speak briefly about that heretic, with your leave. If we consider it rightly, we shall have another Jan Hus on our hands,[67] and we can make an immortal name for ourselves if we burn him on the stake like Hus. But we must be circumspect and keep our eyes open; even in the Council of Constance our predecessors were teachers of heretical pravity, and there were heretics even in our Dominican order, who burned him out of mere envy, using force, fraud, and deceit, breaking accords, perjuring themselves, neglecting and disregarding all laws.[68] These plots are now known to many and they write about it in their books so that we cannot conceal the matter any longer. And so what Hus said in the last days of his life came true, for when he was surrendered to the secular arm for execution, he said: "After a hundred years you will recognize the nature of my teaching, and the truth will come out."[69] A hundred years have gone by more or less, and he has come to life and all his books are in print, and if we are not blinder than moles, we must confess among ourselves that an injustice was done in his case and that our forefathers who burned him were heretics. So we must go about the present business in another way, but I hardly dare to speak out.

HOOGSTRATEN: Speak out boldly. No harm will come to you. We are assembled here under pledge of secrecy—everyone can say what he wants. But don't talk so loud, like a peasant. Lower your voice a little, in case someone is hiding in the stove and listening in.

STENTOR: You have written a book about inquiring into the doctrine of the heretics, in which you proceed according to the old manner, that is, of the Realists and Thomists, and say that a heretic when he justifies and defends himself must not be heard. He must be asked only whether or not he believes in the Roman church. If he does, good. If not, he is burned at the stake—even if he is St. Paul or an angel from heaven. Indeed, if all the old doctors came to life again and didn't believe in the Church, they ought to be burned immediately.[70] But one thing I don't like and can only wonder about: why are you still willing to defend the Roman curia, after the Roman pope relieved you of your duties as inquisitor of heretical depravity, after you suffered defeat in the Reuchlin case,[71] so that all hate you and schoolboys who don't know who you are think, when they hear "Hoogstraten," that it is the devil's name. It would be understandable, if you were entitled to hold a benefice, like our Professor Eck. He achieved something with his ranting and carrying on like a beast, because when he recently returned from the city, the pope gave him five hundred florins and a very fat benefice. That's what I call biting the ear and stroking the tail. So what if he became notorious among scholars and was regarded by them as an ass—he didn't care. But you are a poor monk and mendicant. I'll give you a different piece of advice: Have you never heard that gifts corrupt and blind the eyes even of the wise man?[72]

HOOGSTRATEN: I have always been so busy with St. Thomas that I've never had time to read the bible.

STENTOR: That is not right. Do it now, because we cannot defeat them in any other way except by quoting from Holy Writ. They reject everything else. And another thing: You must write to the pope and ask him to give Luther a cardinalate or a bishopric, and you'll see how quickly he will be silent and retract everything.

HOOGSTRATEN: I fear, Luther will not accept that, because that's too obvious and would cause a great scandal for him. Yet I believe that the Supreme Pontiff would gladly give him not only a cardinalate but even two or three bishoprics if he didn't speak out against the indulgences and against the pope's avarice.

STENTOR: If that doesn't work, we are done for—that's certain. I can't think of any other advice.

HOOGSTRATEN: I should go on with my questioning, but the rest of our colleagues are not here. The majority is present, and thus I wish to draw up a conclusion in accordance with the views of those present. And if I have understood you correctly, no one approves of Luther or the other poets and writers, even though everyone has different proposals. And since at present we cannot examine and rebut all their books, we wish to take no further action at present except to prohibit through letters and public decrees passed by our great university anyone from reading those storytellers. In the meantime, let each one of you be on guard and do what he can at home, examining the books of the poets and writing everything down in a volume. In three months we shall meet again and collect the individual opinions into one volume and publish it with quotations and annotations of St. Thomas in the margin. Let whoever makes derogatory remarks about our council which is lawfully constituted in the Holy Spirit or criticizes it as inappropriate, incur the wrath of the omnipotent God and the Holy Roman See, which is in Babylon, in Satan's synagogue.[73]
Mr. Beadle, read the resolution.

★ ★ ★

RESOLUTION: In the name of the Lord, Amen. By the authority of our most holy lord, Pope Leo X, and the other holy bishops who founded and instituted our great universities of Cologne and Louvain and supported them with privileges, we, the professors of Cologne and Louvain, decree that no one shall read, either publicly or privately, in our exalted university, which is the mother of all German universities, and in the schools of the theologians anything of those new doctrines which have emerged by the counsel of the devil and have led many astray. Furthermore, that they must not speak of them or write of them in letters or any other place; and that the booksellers must not import or sell them to our students; and that the religious houses must not place any of those books in their libraries, on penalty of four golden marks each time they are caught. Those who act contrary to this regulation shall be expelled from universities here and everywhere and in all reputable places for being obstinate and rebellious, on penalty of being prevented from graduating, from receiving a theological degree if they have an M.A., from being promoted to the master's degree if they have a B.A. We condemn the doctrine of Luther and his books, we annihilate them and relegate them to the fire together with their author, not withstanding that we do not understand them and cannot refute them because they are based on the authority of the Gospel and the apostles. But because he does not agree with us and founded a new university and draws to himself all students and doesn't show us the honor we deserve as professors, we counter by excommunicating him according to the sentence passed, and he cannot be absolved except by the professors designated for this purpose: Eck, Lee, and Arnold. Dated etc.

★   ★   ★

HOOGSTRATEN: That will be satisfactory. We shall publish it in this form. And this is the end of our transaction. Thanks be to God. Amen.

NOTES

1. Jäger means "hunter" in German; Crotus is the Latin name for the constellation of the Archer.
2. For Hutten and Reuchlin see p. 2.
3. Cf. p. 2.
4. Learned readers of the sixteenth century would have remembered a line

from the poet Ausonius (*The Mosel*, line 69), in which the two words *rubra corallia* are juxtaposed.

5. Translated from the Latin text in *Hutteni Opera omnia*, IV, pp. 575–585.

6. Cf. p. 2.

7. Cf. below, note 55.

8. Cf. below, pp. 88–89.

9. A term of contempt. In his *Defense Against the Cologne Slanderers* (Tübingen, 1513) Reuchlin wrote: "I refuse to call the slanderers at Cologne 'theologians'; they are counterfeit theologians much like counterfeit money. . . . in the following I shall call them by a better name: 'theologists.' "

10. That is, in 1520, during a phase in the Reuchlin affair when it appeared that the scholar would triumph. When the atmosphere in Rome changed, Hoogstraten was reinstated.

11. 1 Cor. 11:19.

12. Martin Luther.

13. Luke 3:17.

14. Below called "Duplicius," suggesting both duplicity and undecidedness. Perhaps Maarten van Dorp, a Louvain theologian, is hiding under this pseudonym. He was lampooned in a contemporary satire under the name "Phenacus," that is, "Doubledealer," and was characterized by Zwingli as "more versatile than an actor" for switching his support back and forth between humanists and theologians. See also below, note 18.

15. Customary title of Thomas Aquinas, who epitomizes the Realist position in medieval theology.

16. A reference to a popular story about Hoogstraten, recounted, for example, by Erasmus: "One day there appeared at his monastery a knight with a fearful great beard, who glowered at them and demanded to speak with Hoogstraten. The brethren said he was not at home. The knight insisted. They said, no, he wasn't there, but they would give him a message. 'That criminal,' said the knight, 'has attacked in print my noble kinsman, the count of Neuenahr, and he shall pay for it. I give you solemn warning not to set foot on my estates . . . to collect cheese. A thrashing is all you'll get!' " (*Ep.* 877:20–26 [CWE]), with some changes.

17. Virgil, *Eclogues* 10.19.

18. A similar view is expressed by the Louvain theologian Maarten van Dorp, who wrote to Erasmus in 1515: "I know you think that a knowledge of Greek is necessary for my own studies and therefore urge me to acquire it . . . but on this point I disagree with you freely. . . . What prevents me from understanding the Scriptures without Greek?" (*Ep.* 347:361–74 [CWE]). By 1517 Dorp had changed his mind: "How mad of me not to have struggled tooth and nail against the growth of any horrible suspicion that I might be the sort of person to stand against a man like yourself" (*Ep.* 1044:44–47 [CWE]).

19. Dorp was sharply attacked by Erasmus' friends and eventually wrote an anxious letter to Erasmus, asking him to advertise his complete submission: "May I beg you, when you have a suitable opportunity, to mention me somewhere in a friendly way, so that everyone may see that we are in complete agreement" (*Ep.* 1044:57–59 [CWE]).

20. Standard scholastic authors from the fourteenth and fifteenth centuries.

21. Edward Lee (d. 1544) was at that time a student at Louvain. He felt slighted by Erasmus, who had asked him to comment on his New Testament edition. According to Lee, Erasmus belittled his queries but then made use of them in his revised edition without giving him credit. See also note 26 below.

22. Traditional title given to Duns Scotus, the principal exponent of Nominalist theology. Humanists often punned on his name, calling him Mr. Dark (from Greek *skotos*, darkness) because of his complex sentence structure and use of newly coined technical terminology.

23. Lee's ignorance is lampooned. The Church Fathers Jerome, Augustine, and Athanasius, whom he calls "new" are of course older than his idol, Duns Scotus; the charge of introducing changes and innovations was a standard accusation brought against humanists and reformers.

24. Humanists were habitually called "poets" by the theologians because of what appeared to them extravagant language.

25. A work by Peter Lombard, required reading for theology students.

26. Lee accused Erasmus of "falsifying" the New Testament because he omitted the so-called Comma Johanneum from 1 John 5:7 since he had not found it in the Greek manuscripts and therefore considered it an interpolation. This caused an uproar among theologians, who considered the passage one of the most effective prooftexts against Arianism.

27. I.e., the Vulgate, the current Latin version of the New Testament, which was subsequently designated as the standard text for expounding to the faithful by the Council of Trent.

28. The Vulgate version was widely ascribed to Jerome, a theory that was rightly questioned by the humanists. The pun *pervertere* (literally "translates right through," metaphorically "corrupt") cannot be reproduced in English.

29. In a letter to Erasmus (*Ep.* 1061), Lee claimed that a passage in Erasmus' colloquy *The Profane Feast* was aimed at him. The passage runs:

—What good are such writings?
—Good for wrapping fish . . . and wiping your ass.
—I know a scoundrel, whose tongue I'd rather use for this purpose.

Scoundrel (*ardelio* in Latin) was spelled *arde-leo*, a pun on Lee's name.

30. Virgil, *Eclogues* 3.93.

31. Lee's *Annotations . . . on Erasmus' Annotations on the New Testament* were published at Paris in February 1520.

32. Adrian of Utrecht, chancellor of the University of Louvain, who later became Pope Adrian VI.

33. I.e., Erasmus' translation of the New Testament, which diverged from the Vulgate, and had therefore generated a great deal of controversy. Erasmus had so far published two editions, in 1516 and 1519. He was now working on a third, to be published in 1522.

34. In 1507 Hoogstraten had published a refutation of the opinions of Pietro Tomasi of Ravenna (Petrus Ravennas).

35. Cf. p. 2.

36. Johann Maier of Eck (1486–1543), one of the most vocal opponents of Luther; he was a graduate of Cologne, and at this time, teaching at the University of Ingolstadt.

37. Eck was known for his use of body language. Jacob Ziegler described his style of preaching in a letter to Erasmus (*Ep.* 1260:81–2 [Allen]): "He tossed his head, swayed back and forth, and gestured with his hands, counting the points of his argument on his fingers."

38. Matt. 22:15.

39. By Peter of Spain, cf. note 61 below.

40. Johannes Tinctor, the fifteenth-century Cologne theologian.

41. The Bursa Cucana (or Kuijk), a student residence at Cologne.

42. Fourteenth-century Scotists.

43. Mnemonic names for types of syllogisms, but "Berbelin" should be "Barbara" and "Braca" should be "Baroco"—i.e., Eck does not know his syllogisms very well.

44. Eck had just published a book *On the Primacy of the Pope, Against Luther.*

45. Bankers in Augsburg known to finance the purchase of church offices; synodal codicils are letters announcing church appointments.

46. Cf. Luther's letter to Pope Leo X (1520): "The Roman church, once the most holy of all, has become the most licentious den of thieves."

47. Giulio de' Medici. The election of his cousin, Giovanni de' Medici, as Pope Leo X in March 1513 had led to his rapid promotion, first to archbishop (in May), then to cardinal (in September).

48. Perhaps the Dominican Sylvester Prierias, Master of the Sacred Palace.

49. The author is mocking Eck's physique. He is described by an eyewitness of the Leipzig debate as "a heavy and square-set fellow."

50. I.e., the emperor, Charles V, here called "Catholic Monarch," a title inherited from his grandparents, Isabella and Ferdinand of Spain, whose heir he was.

51. Presumably "Derthusian" (as above note 32), that is, Adrian of Utrecht, who had been Charles's tutor and from 1516 on one of his regents in Spain.

52. In 1519 Count Neuenahr, an avid supporter of the Reformation, had published a *Letter of the Champions of Germany to the Emperor Charles.*

53. Arnold of Tongeren or Tungern (d. 1540) obtained his doctorate from the University of Cologne in 1509 and taught there for the next twenty years. He was a fierce anti-Reuchlinist. Pfefferkorn dedicated one of his polemics to Tongeren.

54. Matt. 5:13.

55. The Dominican position, opposed by the Franciscans. To discredit the Franciscans, the Dominicans of Bern staged apparitions of the Virgin declaring in favor of their position. When the fraud was uncovered, those responsible were burned at the stake in 1509. See headnote, p. 55.

56. 2 Cor. 11:14.

57. See note 55 above.

58. A derogatory name. In Latin *scropha* means "breeding sow."

59. A character named Lupold also appears in Pseudo-Hutten's *Hochstratus ovans*; he describes himself as Hoogstraten's right-hand man and relates that he wrote "libellous pamphlets" against the Bishop of Spires who had rendered judgment in Reuchlin's favor.

60. Prov. 22:28.

61. Peter of Spanheym may be Peter of Spain, later Pope John XXI (d. 1277); Tartaretus is Petrus Tartaretus, a contemporary theologian at Paris and author of several commentaries on Aristotle; the *Copulata* was a shortened version of Peter of Spain's *Summulae*, published, according to the title page, "by the professors of Cologne in the Bursa Montis" (Cologne: Quentell, 1496).

62. Philip Melanchthon (1494–1560), eventually to become Luther's right-hand man, was at the time teaching Greek at the University of Wittenberg. Melanchthon, whose scholarly work was impressive and would earn him the title *Praeceptor Germaniae,* "teacher of Germany," had just published his *Rhetoric* (Wittenberg, 1519) and *Brief Instruction in Dialectic* (Wittenberg, 1520).

63. For the *Copulata* and Tartaretus see above, note 61; Bricot may be Edmund Birkhead (Bricotus), Bishop of St. Asaph (d. 1518), who attacked Erasmus' edition of St. Jerome.

64. Stentor, a character in Homer's *Iliad*, was known for his loud voice.

65. Hoogstraten lapses into the vernacular here. The pun *unlauter* (unlutheran/unclean) cannot be reproduced in English.

66. Cf. Exod. 1:9 ff.

67. The Bohemian Jan Hus, who had been condemned to the stake at the Council of Constance in 1415; during a visit to Rome in 1520, Eck had branded Luther the "Saxon Hus."

68. Cf. Luther's defense of Hus at the Leipzig debate in 1519: "Among the articles of Jan Hus I find many that are plainly Christian and evangelical, which the universal Church cannot condemn." He questioned the verdict of the Council of Constance, which had condemned Hus. Eck answered Luther: "If you reject the Council of Constance, if you say a council, legitimately constituted, errs and has erred, you are in my eyes a gentile and a publican."

69. Hus is also reported to have said that they could burn "the goose" (Hus means "goose" in Bohemian), but a swan would appear who would carry out his program. This swan was said to be Luther.

70. In fact Jäger is quoting from his own book, in which he lampoons Hoogstraten's inquisitorial activities, *A solemn tract concerning the art and manner of inquiring into heresy, according to the custom of the Roman Curia . . . written by a certain Brother of Our Dominican Order.* Its place of publication was given as Cologne, Bursa Kneck.

71. Reuchlin had been acquitted, but Hoogstraten was appealing the case to Rome. See p. 2.

72. Cf. 1 Kings 8:3.

73. Luther repeatedly likened Rome to Babylon, e.g., "the Jerusalem that kills the prophets, the purple Babylon" (M. Luther, *Werke* [Weimer: Böhlau, 1883], XIV, p. 445).

4

The Great Lutheran Fool

THOMAS MURNER was born in 1475 in Oberehnheim in Alsace. His family moved to Strassburg, where, at the age of fifteen, he entered the Franciscan order. Between 1495 and 1506 he traveled widely and studied at no fewer than seven universities across Europe, obtaining an M.A. from the University of Paris (1499) and a doctorate in theology from the University of Freiburg (1506). Resuming his studies some ten years later in Basel, he obtained a doctorate in law from that university. In 1520 he returned to Strassburg.

A prolific and many-talented writer, Murner published more than fifty works on pedagogical, historical, and theological subjects. In 1506 he was crowned poet laureate by Maximilian I—an honor richly deserved by the author of the first German verse translation of Virgil's *Aeneid*. His translations from the Latin also include German versions of Henry VIII's *Defense of the Seven Sacraments* and of Justinian's law code.

From 1520 on, Murner became increasingly involved in religious controversies, using his sharp pen in the service of the Catholic church. He had originally been sympathetic toward the reformers' efforts to eliminate clerical abuse, but he drew the line at doctrinal changes and became an indefatigable critic of Luther and Zwingli.

When Strassburg turned Protestant and formally disbanded all monasteries, the Franciscan Murner received a pension and settled as a secular priest in Lucerne. His opposition to the Reformation made him *persona non grata*, however, and when Zwinglianism triumphed, he was forced to flee the city. He returned to his native town, where he remained until his death in 1537.

Murner stands out among the champions of the old faith for his effective use of satire, a weapon more often found in the Protestant camp. *The Great Lutheran Fool* (1522), a poem of almost five thousand verses, is his most ambitious effort in this genre. It is remarkable, not only for its epic length, but also for the author's self-effacing sense of humor. His critics had nicknamed him "Murmauw," that is, "Purrer," and he therefore represented himself in the poem as a cat in a monk's cowl. The feline monk battles the Great Fool, but eventually concludes a truce with him and marries Luther's daughter, only to discover that she is disfigured by the mange. The grotesque plot combines moralizing speeches with slapstick humor, religious instruction with popular entertainment. Taking up Murner's challenge on behalf of the Lutherans, Pamphilus Gengenbach wrote an equally grotesque response, entitled *Novella* (1523). It features a sacristan defending Luther, a parish priest condemning him, a spirit who turns out to be the Lutheran Fool, and Murner who is called to exorcise him. The contorted plot ends with the spirit devouring Murner, thus vividly representing the author's message that the Reformation will triumph and overwhelm its Catholic opponents.

The following excerpts come from the first half of Murner's *Lutheran Fool* in which the cat exorcises a swarm of fools infesting the Great Fool's body.[1] They represent Luther's followers. The Fool's head is infested with the intellectual leaders of the reform movement who question church doctrine, in particular the primacy of the pope and the nature of the sacraments, and who advocate the principle of *sola scriptura*. In the Fool's pockets are those who protest against the church's wealth. Eberlin's *Fifteen Confederates* (see pp. 78–82 and notes 32 and 36 below) also put in an appearance, advocating the dissolution of monasteries, the democratic selection of priests, the use of the vernacular for theological tracts to make them accessible to the common man, and the destruction of images in churches—reform ideas that were now beginning to be implemented.

PREFACE

Thomas Murner, doctor of scriptural studies and both laws, hail to all readers of this book and friendly greetings:

Respected, honorable, and pious reader, of whatever estate and rank, secular or ecclesiastic! I hope you are aware and well acquainted with two of Martin Luther's intentions: first, to reform many things in our holy Christian faith; second, to deal with the many clerical abuses and bring about an improvement—by means right or wrong, I shall not discuss at present. But since such reformation of our Christian faith displeased both me and many others as being in our opinion against God, Holy Writ, and all law and custom, I thought I would serve the cause and promote an understanding of the truth by standing up against him personally, observing however Christian modesty, regard for honor, and respect for individuals. I have therefore published several booklets against him,[2] leaving the final verdict to a general Christian council or to the authorities of our faith, that they may examine argument and counterargument and decide on the truth. As for Luther's intentions to deal with abuses, I have always protested and expressly stated that it was in my opinion useless to deny, justify, or cover up abuses, for it is well understood that the business of holy faith must not be mixed up with human vice or abuse.

Since, then, the business of our faith concerns the whole Christian community, of which I, too, God willing, am a member, I thought I had, by virtue of my Christian freedom, an obligation to speak up. I never expected that this should or would give offense either to Luther or to anyone else on earth, but thought and be-

lieved all the while that discussion would bring out and clarify the
truth and that only untruth suffers no discussion for fear that its
conceit may come to light. My objection was answered by Martin
Luther in a book specifically addressed to me[3] in a tone much like
the impassioned Dido's address to Aeneas on his departure;[4] he
gave my writings a poor reception and answered them with lies
and abuse and a satirical perversion of my family name,[5] something I had never expected from a Doctor and a cleric. Other hap-
less authors did the same under pseudonyms,[6] no doubt to please
him. They disgraced and incriminated me before the whole of
Germany, making me out to be the pope's fiddler,[7] changing me
into a cat and a dragon,[8] depicting me in woodcuts and paintings
with underpants in my hands.[9] Accordingly there is no part of my
body, I believe, that they have not commented on and described,
alluding to everything I have done from the cradle. I hoped to
prove my innocence, as is my privilege, but I am powerless before
the tongues of these mountebanks. I thought they might desist on
their own account, but they have started all over again, making me
out a great and powerful fool,[10] knowing well that if they depicted
me as a clever man their printers would not make half as much
money selling me. Nowadays there must be a monk in every
play,[11] even if he has to be painted in, and I see clearly that I must
be the monk in this play, so that their Lutheran fun and frolic may
not suffer from the lack of a monk. Although I would prefer to be
wise and stay out of this business, I will submit and be that "Murnar," that is, Murner-fool, for which they take me[12] and as they
describe me to all Germany. In the role they have assigned to me I
shall make my defense, which is my right by nature as much as
theirs, who slander me anonymously and in the face of all truth.
But I beg everyone by God and the Virgin—I know of no more
powerful oath or earnest request—not to consider this a frivolous
book, for I am well aware myself that this would not be in keeping
with my profession and my honor. But since nothing can rescue
my honor—neither truth, nor papal decree, nor imperial edict, nor
the verdict of the whole Roman empire—but in defiance of them
all I am made out a powerful and great fool and the pope's fiddler,
I will adapt myself to the time and marketplace[13] and play that
great and powerful fool, perform my role and wear my fool's cap
to say what otherwise would have to be inferred. I hope moreover

His complaint

that the pope, my lord, will thank his fiddler and, since they have pressed me into the fool's role, I shall put away all my wit and ingenuity. Thus I reach for the fool's scepter, and if I strike anyone in an unseemly fashion, he must not complain, for if they had left me alone they need not have suffered this and more from me. It is well said, that one must not overdo the fool.

Finally I beg all men of respectable, honest, and wise estate, clerical or secular, not to fret or worry over this book, for it is written with a fool's wisdom, not with the intention of hurting anyone, but in response to the Lutheran fool- and monkey-books, so that the authors may see themselves in this book as in a mirror holding up to them the awkward and boorish manner in which they go about their fool's business.

Mirror of the Protestants.

HOW THE GREAT LUTHERAN FOOL MUST BE EXORCISED WITH POWERFUL WORDS
(lines 162–173, 190–215)

[THE CAT:] It is now fourteen years[14] that I have been exorcising little fools all by myself, but now we have come to the final hurdle: exorcising the Great Fool. It is certainly a misfortune that in my old days I must slide from the frying pan into the fire.[15] I thought my troubles were over, only to find that a great fool has come into our land, as tall as St. Christopher in the hospital, that is, almost 30 ells tall.[16] . . . As soon as I saw that great pompous fool coming, I fled into a corner and hid, making the sign of the cross—although blessing oneself before a fool is like standing still in a storm[17]—and I bravely called out the three words *Narrabo, Narrabis, Narrabitis*.[18] As soon as I had spoken these three words and exclaimed *Luthery!* I felt refreshed in my heart and mind and soon called on God to protect me from the great fool who came careening here on his sleigh.[19] And finally I remembered that I was an exorcist of fools and had exorcised fools before, though never so great a fool as came rushing toward me through the snow.

WHY THE FOOL IS SO LARGE AND BULGING
(lines 329–355)

[THE GREAT FOOL:] In the Trojan Horse,[20] which was wonderfully large indeed, there never were so many Greeks as there are fools

in me. Why I'm so large I'll tell you now—text, gloss, and all—
for I'm not bulging without reason. Many a fool has burrowed his
way into me; many a fool, who wants to remain nameless, lies
buried within me. Hidden within me, they rest content, without
a care. But if they knew how harshly I was treated with exorcism,
by God, they would sit up and take notice. As it is, they rest content within me, and I know not what to do. Betraying them would
be blasphemy, for "To his guest the host is God."[21] And so I'm
helpless, suffering a grim burden. But the words *Narrabo, Narrabis,
Narrabitis*[22] are too much for me. Each word is breaking my
heart—the devil must have invented them!

THE FOOLS THAT SIT IN THE GREAT FOOL'S HEAD AND
HURT HIM SORELY
(lines 590–652)

[THE GREAT FOOL TO THE CAT:] O dearest cousin, dearest, go gently! But since you are unyielding and vex me with harsh words (no
devil has ever been harder pressed than I), by God, I will discover
where each fool has taken up his lodging, and be quick about it,
so that in your great wisdom you may find each one in his seat.
For each of my limbs, I tell you, has its own fool-tenant. In my
head, which is for thinking, the scholarly fools have taken up their
place—they who preach from the pulpit that they will not let go
of Luther, for they are too fond of him, that he says nothing but
what can be found in the Gospel[23]—the truth for all the world.
(May God grant the truth to all who are without it. Let their
speech be without fail gospel speech and let their teaching be the
gospel word.) But these men look for trouble in this gift and twist
it into trouble, shunning all other teachings of Christ. All they do
is spread slander and polish the Bundschuh[24] and stir up unrest
among the peaceful Christian people.

    The first thing they preach is how to harm the pope and how to
understand *pasce oves meas,*[25] for from these words (they say) one
may judge whether Christ appointed the pope. They want to remove the pope, the shepherd of Christendom, and are hoping for
his downfall. This would be grievous for the sheep, for when the
shepherd has been struck down, the sheep have lost their leader.[26]

Next, they bring up the question why the pope denies you communion in both kinds,[27] the flesh and blood of Christ, as if to tell you that it is done through spite and malice, as if the priests begrudged this to you and with devious lies cheated you of it in a most un-Christian manner. Believe me, no one uses pretense to deprive you of the sacrament. Call me dishonest, if there is a word in all this that can be found in the Gospel—and yet they claim they want to make you devout. They never cite the divine word without twisting it fatally. Thus they prepare the Bundschuh[28] and season it with red cabbage and vinegar—a wonderful mess, and they are licking their fingers. That's what those foolish buffoons like to eat!

THE FOOLS IN THE GREAT FOOL'S POCKETS
(lines 698–770)

[THE GREAT FOOL:] There are fools sitting in my pockets, who would love to get their hands on the money and property of others and have a good time with it. There are fools sitting in my pockets, who are waiting for goods and money. Strange fellows they are, who would like someone to play the part of the robber for them, so that they could get their hands on the property of another. They are the ones who sit in my pockets here. They have their own gospel, how to reverse donations and destroy monasteries[29]—that is the gospel they preach industriously. This is how they would happily distribute goods and money. By God, a golden life! Their gospel declares that the clergy should go begging from house to house forever, as Christ himself did. Take off two of the pope's crowns[30] and leave him only one for decoration!

O hungry gnats, how you bite! All the traditions started by our bishops you want to do away with. Their tithe, their possessions that allow them to lead a rich and splendid life, you want to take for yourselves. You want to do away with cardinals and take from the pope the Donation of Constantine.[31] The clergy must not have castles, cities, and land! they say. This is not their true opinion, but they pretend it is and tell you how they will share the clerical income with their fellow man: first of all they will give money to the hospitals and to the sick, and they are full of pity for the city's

homeless, widows, and orphans.[32] What they don't admit is that
they are selling the bearskin before they've gone hunting. God
does not allow anyone to steal and rob—why, then, should one
person take what another owns by right and title? They have made
up a pretense so that the common people won't see through and
will think it must be a Christian doctrine, whereas it is a lie. If
they really took all the possessions and put them on a heap, the
poor would fare as they did in Bohemia.[33] There also the poor
thought that they would get their proper share of the loot, but the
rich took it and left the poor to comfort themselves as best they
could in their misery.

I am not very old and I remember that a Bundschuh had come
together on the Hungersberg.[34] They too thought they would
share in the land, but they were tied to the wheel and tortured.
One man, whose name was Ulman,[35] was tried at Basel, and
rightly so, for taking a share of another's property. Thieves and
robbers always come to a bad end.

THE FOOLS IN THE GREAT FOOL'S BELLY
(lines 771–792)

[THE GREAT FOOL:] I am pregnant with great fools. I wish they
were pilloried and left floating in the ocean, if only I could get rid
of them. O cousin dear, if only you knew why my belly is swol-
len. You would be surprised how many fools are in there together
and that such a number would want to be there. Ah, if you could
drive them out, you would do me a great service. I cannot suffer
them much longer. I am waiting for you to invent some kind of
exorcism. I cannot feed them any longer. Your exorcism has been
so hard on me that I want to betray them. There are altogether
fifteen of them, though none of them has a name. They are big,
fat fellows and are called the Fifteen Confederates.[36]

[The confederates are called forth to explain their mission.]

THE SECOND CONFEDERATE
(lines 916–952)

I want to abolish fasting,[37] for my good grey horse died of it, and
I have much experience in this matter. If one does not leave fodder

for a horse and has the poor creature fast too long, letting it nibble
at an empty crib, it loses weight and bulk so that one can count
the ribs. Will not a human being lose weight when a beast does?
Fasting must be done away with. Even an iron ox would die of it.
Will not then a man made of flesh die and perish of long fasting?
. . . Why should we ask the pope's opinion on what to put down
our throats when our stomachs rumble. Why run to Rome[38] to get
eggs, butter and cheese? We'll be dead of starvation before we can
make it back. The wolf doesn't ask Rome's permission to feed on
a sheep from the herd or a chicken from the coop. He eats meat
even during Lent. Should a wolf have more freedom than a pious
Christian? I don't understand it. Let the pope lord it over wolves!

THE THIRD CONFEDERATE
(lines 969–1011)

I am the third who embellishes the ranks of the fools and leads
their parade. No need to bless yourselves. I'm here on behalf of
the nuns, for a good tumble does more for you than a virginal
mind.[39] Why should a nun be penned up like a sow? Why should
she rot in her own juices? Better give them a tanning! Why shut
them up? Leather wants tanning! Everything looks for its due and
wants recognition. In this matter I follow the example of the wolf
who said to the shepherd: "My dear shepherd, why do you hole
up your sheep and keep them confined to this narrow pen? They
are all going to suffer from cramps. Let them run, so they won't
go lame from all this standing around. I am not speaking on my
own behalf. I am begging you on behalf of those poor sheep." Just
so I feel sorry for those poor girls shut up in nunneries. Let them
take a look around and see the world a bit. Perhaps they'll find
someone agreeable to make babies with. Let them romp a little
and stuff their hindquarters. Bring them to Blumers and Baden[40]
or their wombs will dry up. Dear God, release the poor girls; they
are of flesh and blood like us. I speak on their behalf, or else I
wouldn't lift a finger. When they have had their fun and have
romped with fresh young fellows, let them go back to their nunneries.

THE EIGHTH CONFEDERATE
(lines 1260–1315)

The band wouldn't be complete without me. Or else who would explain why we must write everything in German or any other language except Latin?[41] I shall explain it to you neatly. We have read in old books that our cousins a long time ago were of the German order; that's why we began to write in German. If we taught in Latin, no one in the land would know what great fools we are and few people would be aware of our existence. Also, when we write in German, the printers make a profit selling the books and fill their wallets, which doesn't harm us either. Also, in the German language we can express ourselves satirically and ridicule other writers, as we did with Murner in *Karsthans*.[42] And there are many German words that defy Latinization. For example, how could we render 'Murmauw'[43] in Latin . . . or 'stick-in-the mud' or 'doughboy' or 'shorn mug' and other such expressions? They exist in German, but they can't be translated into Latin. That's why we write in German, so that every village butcher can have one of our books, which are published for the benefit of Christians. Thus the common people can learn from them and name the twelve apostles and think of us at the inn when they drink their wine, mulling over the new Christian state described by the Confederates.[44] Also, being clever chaps, we didn't want to share this with the French.[45] If we had written in Latin, it would be theirs to read. That's why we wrote in German, so that it'll stay in Germany.

(Ah, I wish it had been written in the pigs' troughs so that it might stay with the pigs. Then there would not be strife and dissension everywhere as is the custom and tradition of fools.)

THE ELEVENTH CONFEDERATE
(lines 1425–1482)

What can we do about the authorities, the pope and the emperor? Now that we have taken the matter in hand and reformed the clergy and burned the rights of the church, let us bring order and reform to the secular state. We need no help from the emperor

Every man will be turned loose to his own devices

here—although we wouldn't want anyone to think that we do not want an emperor. We couldn't pass him over; there would be too much resistance. His authority and power is too great. He would soon give us more trouble than twenty fools could bear. So take care not to complain. Instead we'll draw up statutes[46] and keep them confidentially among us—statutes to govern the whole secular state.

Democracy?

Pope and cardinals, priests and monks we'll cast out. We piss on them.[47] Each parish, each community is to have one elected priest. The man they like best shall be their priest. They'll give him a wife and enough pay and gold to have his fill.[48] And in case of illness he'll have a chaplain who will personally sing in the women's chapel,[49] for the chapel wants a saint and cannot be without a singer on the feastday. And each village has its parish priest just as it has its bull.[50] As the cowherd is with his cows, so the chaplain joins any unmarried woman in the village who requests his services. Indeed it is his obligation to earn his bull-fee[51] and do his task well and have no woman complain. God himself has made you monks and monkeys.[52] God has given you this freedom in baptism. And just as the priest has his place and cows have a bull, you must elect a good boar[53] to mount the sows—and no man shall interfere with him.

THE FOURTEENTH CONFEDERATE
(lines 1595–1632)

I want to speak of the saints,[54] their lives and times. I'll teach the Christian people how to venerate them. If you encounter cheap tin saints, don't bother to venerate them. I have a rule that has never failed me: base coin for base funeral Masses. But I do like wooden saints, even if there were twelve thousand of them: they come in handy as firewood. The stone saints I leave alone. Many saints are harmful to Christians. One shouldn't fast for a saint. How can he be holy when he denies me my wine and takes the bread out of my mouth as if I were a dog? I do praise St. Martin—he gives us geese with our wine.[55] . . . other feast days I find are not well arranged. I am thinking of the saints whose names come up on the calendar in winter time. They should be switched to summer so

Iconoclast. Despoiling me, metals they are made of

that we won't have to suffer the cold. I am not complaining about
the helpers in need, those who are made of gold and silver and are
standing in the churches. We need them indeed. They are no doubt
a help to us Christians, especially once we have changed them into
cash.

How the Unknown and Hidden Karsthans Was Rooted Out with a Strong Laxative and Potion
(lines 2631–2712)

[THE CAT:] Now let all bells ring in these times of joy, for through
magic and medication the learned Karsthans has been uncovered,
who has so far been unknown. It's great reading. There is no lack
of people to laugh at his words or tell the jokes to others. He
knows how to be fun. If the emperor knew who he was, he would
make him a great man, for he can tell such pretty tales. All books
there are on earth should be modeled after his. His book would
make a great model, into which all books should be poured as if
it were a motherlode from which fresh ones are born. I am im-
pressed, upon my oath! That's why I am so sorry that he was
found in your behind. He should have had a more honorable abode
than a fool's bowels, from which he could be driven out easily and
flushed out back. Fie, how shameful that Karsthans[56] should be
shat, that the noble poet with his book should pass through the
Fool's shit. I am a cat and lack reason; that's why I use coarse
words. If I had been given a human nature, I would not utter
coarse words. O cousin, dearest cousin mine, I cannot but be angry that you did not give a more honorable place to Karsthans,
that you did not have better sense than letting him dwell in your
behind. He deserved a better reward for his writing.

[THE GREAT FOOL:] O dear cousin, don't be angry and please hear
my explanation. He sat together with the other fools and I was
certainly mindful of him; but he was told that he was wanted[57] and
that an ordinance had been published that anyone writing invectives should get his just deserts, as is written in the imperial law
leaving no excuse or objection: he must go from the gallows to the
wheel.[58] But it would be a shame if such a craftsman should go to

the gallows and wheel. He meant well and pleased the world and gave them a bellyful of laughs. So when he heard the news that the emperor was angry, he didn't want to wait with the other fools for misery to overtake him, but took refuge in my arse, thus to be freed from all cares. But now he is truly in the hot seat and will be led to the gallows and from that lovely spot[59] to the wheel, so that he will repent and publish no more invectives anonymously, as he did so often before. If you hadn't driven him out, he would have stayed even longer. O dearest cousin mine, let him crawl back. He would be so grateful to you!

THE FOOLS IN THE GREAT FOOL'S EARS
(lines 2786–2836)

O God, what great fools and buffoons sit in my ears. They do not want to hear what is taught on earth, what the Christian community is like and what it teaches, what all the saints teach—all this they do not want to hear. For fifteen hundred whole years they were waiting for the Fool and all the while they were deaf, but now when they read in books that there is no purgatory for their sins,[60] that the prayers of the saints are of no help, that they do not hear us above, that the Mass is no sacrifice,[61] and how the priests much curtail and sift the sacraments until nothing is left, and how confession can be made smoother with a glass of good wine in good company and we might sin thereafter and absolve each other[62]—smear the throat with monkey fat! They can hear Luther clearly, even if they are a thousand miles away, but they cannot hear the preacher in their own city. They can hear two fools whisper and lisp but they cannot hear what all the land, all cities and princes, and the emperor himself advises—they can't hear any of that. They are completely deaf, they cannot hear a word. But they hear very well in other matters: how to be robbers and break into monasteries with a crash—they call it baking Lutheran cookies[63]— and strike until the girders give way and they can fit in their Bund- schuh. Lies will bring it about, for those who hear the truth will leave to each the property he holds by God's will and by rights.

Who knows, perhaps you too will one day hear what you don't want to hear since now you want to hear only what pleases you.

The day will come when God will hear what is to your detriment. Then your deafness will not be forgotten and you'll be taught a lesson on how to open your ears wide.

NOTES

1. Translated from the German text in *Thomas Murners Deutsche Schriften*. IX. *Von dem grossen Lutherischen Narren*, ed. P. Merker (Strassburg: Trübner, 1918).

2. Murner published four pamphlets against Luther in 1520, specifically attacking his denial of papal primacy. Although they appeared anonymously, a postscript emphasized that the author had identified himself to the bishop of Strassburg and obtained a printing privilege.

3. In April 1521 Luther published *Against Emser's Book . . .* , with the subtitle "Mindful also of Murnarrs [i.e., Mur-fool's] book."

4. Virgil, *Aeneid* 4.584ff., where Queen Dido curses her lover, Aeneas, who is about to desert her.

5. See above, note 3.

6. For example, Nicolaus Gerbel in his dialogue *Murnar the Leviathan*, Joachim Vadian in *Karsthans*, which was often ascribed to Hutten (see below, note 57), and Urbanus Rhegius in his *Question and Answer, A dialogue between Symon Hessus and Martin Luther recently held at Worms*, all published in 1521.

7. That is, his toady. Murner is depicted in this form on the title-page of Vadian's *Song of the Wolf*.

8. For example, in Vadian's *Karsthans* and in Gerbel's *Murner the Leviathan*.

9. In 1521 Johann Prüss, a Strassburg printer who supported the Reformation, brought out a new edition of Murner's *Of the Four Dominican Heretics* (cf. below, note 14) prefaced by ironic verses ridiculing the critics of the Reformation and a title-page that depicted Murner as a monk with a cat's head, a dragon's tail, and underpants in his hands (suggesting that he was caught "with his pants down" in an amorous adventure).

10. Apparently an image of Murner as fool had been carried around during carnival. Cf. Murner's allusions at lines 3389–3397 of the *Great Lutheran Fool*, where the troops of the reformers describe their methods: "Then we thought of this device: We gave him a cat's head, but he just laughed and said he liked to eat young mice and was used to headlice. In fact he thanked us for giving him a cat's head. So we sat the great fool in a cart and paraded him around."

11. Cf. the proverbial expression, "Take heed of an ass behind, of a monk on all sides" (*Oxford Dictionary of English Proverbs* [Oxford: Clarendon, 1970], p. 604).

12. Cf. above, note 3.

13. A proverbial expression, meaning "to adapt to the circumstances."

14. Murner's first contribution to the Reformation controversy is *Of the Four Dominican Heretics*, composed shortly after May 1509 (when the event it describes took place).

15. Literally, "from the cart to the wagon," of an animal that is required to pull a heavier load.

16. According to medieval legend, St. Christopher warded off death. Statues

and pictures of the saint were therefore prominently displayed in hospitals. One ell is the equivalent of about twenty-four inches.

17. I.e., useless.

18. Latin words, literally translated, "I shall tell, you [singular] will tell, you [plural] will tell." The words are chosen for their similarity to German *Narr*, "fool."

19. As in a carnival parade, which, being held in February, involved sleighs as floats.

20. According to Homeric legend, the Greeks, after besieging Troy in vain for ten years, entered the city hidden in a wooden horse.

21. I.e., the host is a powerful protector. The expression is proverbial; cf. Erasmus, *Adages* 1.1.69.

22. Cf. above, note 18.

23. The principle of *sola scriptura* (exclusive reliance on Scripture and rejection of church regulations) was adopted by many reformers; thus the generic name "evangelicals" for supporters of the Reformation.

24. Peasant's clog, used as an emblem in the peasant revolts at the turn of the century and again in the Peasants' War of 1525. To "polish" or "twist" (an expression Murner uses at line 678 of his poem) the Bundschuh means to create a disturbance. Luther was depicted polishing the Bundschuh on a contemporary broadsheet (cf. illustration in F. Bezold, *Geschichte der deutschen Reformation* [Berlin: Grote, 1890], p. 361).

25. "Feed my sheep" (John 21:15), the traditional prooftext for those defending papal primacy, a principle attacked by Luther in *On the Papacy* (1520).

26. Cf. Zach. 13:7.

27. Another point of contention between reformers and Catholics; in his *Sermon on the Holy Sacrament* (1519) Luther spoke in favor of communion in both. The practice was widely adopted by the reformers and came to be regarded as a demonstration of adherence to the Lutheran cause.

28. See above, note 24.

29. Monasteries were dissolved where the Reformation succeeded. The inmates were usually compensated, as in Murner's own case (see headnote above), but the process was not without its problems and occasionally issued in violence.

30. A reference to the papal tiara, which was threefold. It was thought to represent the pope's power over earth, heaven, and hell. Murner is obviously suggesting that the reformers wanted to deprive the pope of his earthly domain. Cf. also his reference to the Donation of Constantine (cf. below, note 31).

31. The Donation of Constantine, the historical justification for the pope's territorial claims to the region around Rome, was revealed as a forgery by Lorenzo Valla in the fifteenth century. Ulrich von Hutten brought out a new edition of Valla's *Against the Forged and Fabricated Donation of Constantine* in 1517.

32. In drawing up statutes for an ideal city, Eberlin (see below, note 44) suggested that monasteries be turned into hospices for the old and poor.

33. Murner is referring to events surrounding the Hussite reformation at the beginning of the century, when the estates of monasteries were confiscated only to be appropriated by local gentry. See, for example, D. Whaley, *Later Medieval Europe* (London: Longmans, 1968), pp. 135–39.

34. Near Schlettstadt in Alsace. Murner is referring to a conspiracy in 1493 against the bishop of Strassburg.

35. The mayor of Schlettstadt, who was the head of the conspiracy.

36. The title of a collection of popular reformation tracts by Johann Eberlin. For extracts in translation see Steven Ozment, *The Reformation in the Cities* (New Haven: Yale University Press, 1975), pp. 97–107.

37. Ostentatious violations of the rules of fasting were reported, for example, in Basel, where in 1521 a certain Sigmund Steinschnyder was put to death for serving pork to his guests in Lent (cf. ASD IX–1, 65–66).

38. I.e., to get a papal dispensation from the regulations governing fasting.

39. Discussing the respective values of marriage and celibacy was a literary commonplace, but in light of the reformers' dissolution of monasteries, the question took on new relevance. Erasmus, for example, was berated and attacked in a public lecture for writing a rhetorical exercise, *In Praise of Marriage*, in which he placed marriage above celibacy.

40. German spas, known as much for their holiday spirit as for the healing powers of their springs.

41. Catholic theologians had misgivings about laymen discussing theological matters and objected strongly to discussions among common men who had no scholarly education; the use of Latin assured a certain exclusivity.

42. See above, note 8, and section below, pp. 82–83.

43. See headnote above for this nickname given to Murner.

44. Statutes for an ideal city are drawn up by Eberlin in the Eleventh Confederate, satirized in lines 1425–1482 below.

45. A reference to the traditional rivalry between the Germans and the French which reached a high point shortly before the publication of *The Great Lutheran Fool* with the competition of Francis I and Charles V for the imperial crown in 1519.

46. Eberlin's Tenth and Eleventh Confederate contain statutes purportedly brought by a traveler ("Psittacus," i.e., parrot) from the utopian state "Wolfaria," i.e., the land of well-being.

47. Literally, "we shit into their hearts."

48. In his utopia Eberlin suggested that the priest be a local man and his wife, if possible, a local woman. He is to be elected by the community for life and to receive a salary of two hundred gulden.

49. "A woman's chapel" was a slang expression denoting the female sexual organ.

50. The pun *Pfarrer* (parish priest)/*far* (bull) cannot be duplicated in English.

51. Paid to the owner of a bull for insemination.

52. The pun in German, *Pfaffen/Affen*, i.e., "clerics/monkeys," has no exact equivalent in English.

53. The pun *Eber* (boar)/Eberlin (the author of the *Fifteen Confederates*) cannot be duplicated in English.

54. The objection of reformers to the veneration of saints led to iconoclasm in many cities. See also below, pp. 92–94.

55. St. Martin's feast was celebrated on November 11. It was customary on this day to have roast goose and try out the new wine.

56. The title of Vadian's satire (see above, note 8). The figure of Karsthans represented the typical peasant.

57. Murner may have been thinking of Ulrich von Hutten, to whom *Karsthans* was generally ascribed (cf. note 6 above) and whose printer in Mainz was arrested. Hutten himself was forced to flee the city and take refuge in Franz von Sickingen's fortified castle.

58. I.e., from bad to worse.

59. Literally, *Meyenbad* (a bath in May). The expression is used ironically.

60. In the Ninety-Five Theses Luther asks why, if the pope had jurisdiction over purgatory, he did not abolish it altogether; later, in 1525, Guillaume Farel would declare succinctly: "Purgatory is nothing but an invention of the devil" (*Sommaire*, chap. 19).

61. The reformers regarded the Mass as a memorial service rather than a sacrifice.

62. A reference to the rejection of secret, aural confession and the role of the priest as mediator between the sinner and God by reformers.

63. I have not come across this expression elsewhere. Perhaps a reference to a popular woodcut entitled "Die göttliche Mühle" ("God's Mill"), which shows Luther kneading dough. Cf. the illustration in C. Augustijn, *Erasmus: His Life, Works, and Influence* (Toronto: University of Toronto Press, 1991) n.p.

5

A Journey for Religion's Sake

DESIDERIUS ERASMUS (1469–1536) was perhaps the most widely read Northern humanist. Orphaned at an early age, he was pressured by his guardians to enter a monastery. His intellectual gifts were recognized by his bishop, who sent him to Paris to study theology. However, the scholastic brand of theology taught at the university left Erasmus dissatisfied and he departed without a degree. During the following years he developed his own approach to theology, an approach which relied on the thorough study of Scripture aided by patristic exegesis. Erasmus was also a lover of classical literature. His polished style of writing was much admired by his contemporaries, and his manuals and textbooks—the fruit of his wide reading in the classics and his experience as a tutor in Paris—were widely used. His scholarly career reached its zenith in 1516 when he published a revised and annotated text of the Latin Vulgate Bible, accompanied by the original Greek—the *editio princeps*. The revisions he proposed or implemented caused much controversy and were attacked by theologians who regarded Erasmus as a meddling philologist. They were concerned about the doctrinal implications of the textual changes advocated by him and saw his work as a seedbed of dissension and an inspiration to reformers. Indeed, many of Erasmus' contemporaries regarded him as Luther's forerunner and teacher, a notion vigorously combated by the humanist. Erasmus no doubt shared many of the reformer's concerns, sympathizing in particular with his efforts to do away with ceremonialism and to encourage a more spiritual approach to religion, but he shied away from advocating doctrinal changes or challenging the teaching authority of the church. It was his misfortune to be caught in the firing line between the two camps. Defenders of the old faith found his criticism of the church provocative and his pronouncements suspect, if not unorthodox. They were inclined to disbelieve Erasmus' protestations of loyalty. The champions of reform, who had counted him among their number, thought that he had not been emphatic enough in his criticism of the church and regarded his refusal to break with tradition as a betrayal of their cause and a sign of cowardice.

The following text comes from a work entitled *Colloquies*, a collection of dialogues originally intended to teach schoolboys classical Latin.[1] The material Erasmus added to later editions changed the nature of the work, turning it into a social commentary. The use of satire made these later dialogues particularly effective tools of criticism. Among the pieces that deal with the abuses of the church are "The Funeral," which lashes out against clerics who are more interested in a dying man's will than in his confession; "Shipwreck," which lampoons vows made by superstitious people in distress; "Fish Diet," a protest against fasting and dietary laws; and "A Journey for Religion's Sake," the text of which appears below.

This colloquy, first published in 1526, typifies Erasmus' position midway between conservatives and reformers. On the one hand, he is critical of superstitious pilgrims and lashes out against the custodians of shrines, who serve up old wives' tales to extract donations from gullible visitors. On the other hand, he makes a thinly veiled attack on Ulrich Zwingli and rejects the Swiss reformer's efforts to abolish the practice of venerating saints altogether. The *Colloquies* evoked much protest from the Catholic side. The faculty of theology at the University of Paris, a bastion of the old faith, condemned many of the dialogues as heretical and blasphemous. The official censure prompted Erasmus to add to his next edition a defense entitled "On the Usefulness of the *Colloquies*" in which he insisted that his remarks had been innocuous. He summarized the content and purpose of "A Journey for Religion's Sake" in this manner:

> I reproach men who have wreaked havoc by removing the images of saints from churches, but also those who foolishly go on journeys, pretending that they are undertaken for religion's sake. Indeed clubs are formed for this purpose, and those who have been to Jerusalem are called "golden knights" and address one another as "brothers." On Palm Sunday they solemnly act out a ridiculous scene, dragging a donkey by a rope (themselves being not much different from the wooden donkey they pull). Those who have been to Compostela act similarly. Let us by all means indulge their whims, but let us not allow them to claim holiness on account of these things, for this is intolerable. I also criticize those who display as genuine articles relics of a doubtful provenance, who attribute to them more importance than is proper, and who basely profit from them.[2]

MENEDEMUS:[3] What strange sight is this? Can this be my neighbor Ogygius,[4] on whom no one has laid eyes for six whole months now? Rumor had it that he was dead. Unless I'm dreaming, it's him! I'll go up to him and greet him. Good day, Ogygius!

OGYGIUS: Good day to you, too, Menedemus.

MENEDEMUS: From what corner of the world have you returned to us, safe and sound? A sad rumor was spreading here that you had sailed into the Styx.[5]

OGYGIUS: No, thanks to the gods, I'm feeling better than ever.

MENEDEMUS: I hope you'll always be able to put to rest rumors of this sort. But what's this outfit? You're covered all over with shells and with tin and lead badges, and decked out with necklaces of straw, and there is a rosary snaking around your arm as well.[6]

OGYGIUS: I've visited St. James in Compostela and, on my way back, the famous Virgin-by-the Sea in England[7]—or rather, I re-visited her, for I was there three years ago.

MENEDEMUS: A pleasure trip, I imagine.

OGYGIUS: Oh, no—a journey for religion's sake!

MENEDEMUS: The kind of religion you learn from Greek books,[8] I suppose.

OGYGIUS: My mother-in-law made a vow that, if her daughter gave birth to a healthy baby boy, I'd pay my respects to St. James without delay and thank him in person.

MENEDEMUS: Did you pay your respects to the saint only in your and your mother-in-law's name?

OGYGIUS: No, in the whole family's.

MENEDEMUS: Well, in my opinion, your family would have been no worse off if you had left St. James ungreeted. But tell me, what did he say in reply to your thanks?

OGYGIUS: He didn't say anything, but he seemed to smile and nod his head slightly when I offered my gift, and he held out these shells.

MENEDEMUS: Why does he give out shells rather than something else?

OGYGIUS: Because he has a plentiful supply of shells from the sea nearby.

MENEDEMUS: A well-meaning saint! He delivers women in labor and gives presents to visitors. But what new method of making vows is this? Can a lazy fellow now impose the work on others? If you made a vow that I should fast twice a week if your affairs went well, do you think I'd fulfill your vow?

OGYGIUS: I don't think you would, even if you had sworn it yourself. For you like to make fun of the saints. But she is my mother-in-law and must be obliged. You know how emotional women are, and besides it was in my own interest too.

MENEDEMUS: If you hadn't kept her vow, what risk would you have run?

OGYGIUS: The saint couldn't have sued me, I admit, but he could have played deaf to my prayers thereafter or quietly brought some disaster on my family. You know what the mighty can do.

MENEDEMUS: Tell me, how is the worthy St. James?

OGYGIUS: A great deal colder than usual.

MENEDEMUS: What is the reason? Old age?

OGYGIUS: Nonsense. You know that saints don't grow old. But there is a new conviction swaying the world which results in the saint's being greeted less frequently than usual. And those who do come merely greet him and make only the tiniest donation. They insist the money is better spent on the poor.

Decline in the veneration of saints.

MENEDEMUS: An impious idea!

OGYGIUS: And thus so great an apostle, who used to be resplendent with gold and jewels, stands there, a bare wooden figure with no more than a wax candle.

MENEDEMUS: If what I hear is true, there is danger that the same will happen to other saints.

OGYGIUS: Worse than that: a letter is circulating which the Virgin Mary herself wrote on this subject.

MENEDEMUS: Which Mary?

OGYGIUS: Mary called *A Lapide*.[9]

MENEDEMUS: In Switzerland, unless I am mistaken.

OGYGIUS: That's the one.

MENEDEMUS: To whom did she address the letter?

OGYGIUS: The name of the addressee is on the letter.

MENEDEMUS: And who delivered the letter?

OGYGIUS: No doubt, she sent it through an angel, who placed it on the pulpit where the addressee preaches. And there can be no question about the authenticity of the letter; you can see that it's an autograph.

MENEDEMUS: What—can you recognize the hand of the angel who is the Virgin's secretary?

OGYGIUS: Of course.

MENEDEMUS: But how?

OGYGIUS: I have read Bede's epitaph, which was cut into stone by an angel. The shape of the letters is exactly the same. Also I've read the handwritten message to St. Giles.[10] It's the same hand. Doesn't that prove it sufficiently?

MENEDEMUS: Is one permitted to see the letter?

OGYGIUS: Yes, if you promise to keep silent about it.

MENEDEMUS: Silent like a stone.

OGYGIUS: But there are stones that are notorious for keeping nothing silent.

MENEDEMUS: Like a deaf man, then, if you don't trust stones.

OGYGIUS: On that condition I'll read it to you. Pay attention.

MENEDEMUS: I am.

Zwingli [handwritten annotation]

OGYGIUS: "Mary, Mother of Jesus, to Glaucoplutus,[11] greetings. I would like you to know how deeply grateful I am to you for adopting Luther's views and making every effort to persuade people that the invocation of saints is useless. For up until now I was almost dropping from exhaustion because of the shameless entreaties of mortals. They put all their requests to me alone, as if my Son always remained a baby—seeing that he is portrayed and painted as a child in my lap—as if he still depended on his mother's consent and would not dare to deny anything to a petitioner for fear that if he did deny him anything, I in turn would deny him the breast when he was thirsty. And sometimes they ask me, a virgin, what a decent youth would hardly dare to ask a prostitute—things I am ashamed to put in writing. Sometimes a merchant about to sail for Spain to make a profit commits the chastity of his mistress to me. And a nun who has cast off her veil and is preparing to run away commits to me her reputation for virtue, which she herself intends to sell. A godless soldier, hired to slaughter people, implores me: 'Blessed Virgin, give me lots of loot.' And a gambler cries: 'Favor me, saintly virgin, I'll give you a cut of my winnings!' And if they lose, they abuse and curse me because I didn't favor their wicked game. Someone who pursues a shameful trade cries: 'Give me a fat profit.' If I refuse anything they protest immediately: 'Then you are not the Mother of

The Letter from Mary. [handwritten annotation]

Mercy!' Some people's prayers are absurd rather than impious. An unmarried girl cries: 'Mary, give me a rich and handsome husband.' A married woman cries: 'Give me beautiful kids.' A pregnant woman cries: 'Grant me an easy delivery' and an old woman: 'Give me a long life without a cough or a dry throat.' A crazy old man cries: 'Let me be young again.' A philosopher: 'Give me the ability to devise insoluble, knotty problems.' A priest: 'Give me a rich benefice.' A bishop: 'Save my church.' A sailor: 'Give me a prosperous journey.' A prefect cries: 'Show me your Son before I die.' A courtier: 'Grant that I may confess the truth when I am at the point of death.' A countryman: 'Give me a good downpour.' A country woman: 'Preserve my flock and my herd from harm.' If I deny anything, they declare that I am cruel. If I refer them to my son, I hear: 'Your will is his will.' So am I, a woman and a virgin, all by myself to stand by sailors, soldiers, merchants, gamblers, newlyweds, pregnant women, governors, kings, and farmers? What I've described is a small part of my troubles. But nowadays I'm bothered a great deal less by such matters, for which I am very grateful, except that this advantage has brought with it an even greater disadvantage: I have more leisure, but less honor and wealth. Formerly I was hailed the 'Queen of Heaven, Mistress of the World,' now I scarcely hear a 'Hail Mary' from a few visitors. Formerly I was decked out in gold and jewels, had many different outfits, was honored with golden and jeweled offerings — now I have no more than a short cloak, and that one is mouse-eaten. My annual income is barely enough to support one wretched sacristan to light a little lamp or candle. But these hardships would be bearable if it weren't for a rumor that you are plotting even greater ones. You are trying, they say, to remove everything that has to do with saints from the churches. Just stop and think what you are doing! Other saints don't lack the means of avenging such injury. If Peter is cast out of his church, he can in turn shut you out from heaven. Paul has a sword, Bartholomew a knife. William is fully armed under his monk's robe and carries a heavy lance. And what could you do against George on his horse, clad in his coat of mail, carrying a spear and formidable sword? Anthony is not unarmed either: he has his sacred fire. Other saints likewise have their weapons or can bring misfortune on anybody they please. Although I am unarmed, you shall not cast me out unless you cast out the Son I am holding in my arms together with me. For I shall not be parted from him. Either you cast him out together with me, or you let us both remain here—or do you prefer a church without Christ? This much I wanted you to know. Consider your answer carefully, because this is a matter of grave concern to me.

From my house of stone, on the 1st of August, in the year of my Son's passion, 1524.

I, the blessed Virgin, have signed this with my own hand."

MENEDEMUS: A formidable and threatening letter! I imagine Glaucoplutus will watch his steps.

OGYGIUS: If he is wise.

MENEDEMUS: Why didn't the worthy St. James write to him about this matter as well?

OGYGIUS: I don't know. Perhaps because he is farther away and all letters are intercepted nowadays.

MENEDEMUS: But what god brought you to England?

OGYGIUS: An unexpectedly favorable breeze invited me there, and I had practically promised St. Mary-by-the-Sea that I should visit her again in two years' time.

MENEDEMUS: What were you going to request of her?

OGYGIUS: Nothing out of the ordinary, just the usual: a safe and sound family, more money, a long and happy life in this world and eternal happiness in the next.

MENEDEMUS: Couldn't the Virgin Mother here at home provide you with the same things? Her church in Antwerp is much grander than the one by the sea.

OGYGIUS: I can't deny it, but different blessings are given out in different places, either because it was decreed thus or because she accommodates our prayers, for she is kind.

MENEDEMUS: I've often heard about St. James, but do me the favor of describing the domain of Mary-by-the-Sea.

OGYGIUS: I'll do it as briefly as I can. She enjoys enormous prestige throughout England. Hardly anyone on the island would dare hope for prosperity if he did not greet her with an annual gift, however small, according to his means.

MENEDEMUS: Where does she live?

OGYGIUS: In the far northwest of England, about three miles from the sea. The village derives its livelihood almost exclusively from the pilgrims. There is a college of canons who are called "regular": an order halfway between monks and secular canons.[12]

MENEDEMUS: You mean they are amphibians, like beavers?

OGYGIUS: And crocodiles, yes. But I can't go into details. I'll try to give you a satisfactory explanation in a few words. In unpleasant matters they are canons; in pleasant matters, monks.

MENEDEMUS: So far you are speaking in riddles.

OGYGIUS: Let me give you an example. If the Roman pontiff were to strike all monks with his thunderbolt, they'd be canons, not monks. If he were to permit all monks to take wives, they'd be monks.

MENEDEMUS: Strange privileges—I wish they'd take my wife too.

OGYGIUS: My point is that the college depends almost entirely on the Virgin's generosity for its income, for the larger gifts are kept, but petty cash or anything of small value is used to support the community and their prefect, whom they call prior.

MENEDEMUS: Do they live decent lives?

OGYGIUS: They are not undeserving of praise. They have more devotion than annual income. The church is kept neat and clean, but the Virgin does not dwell in the church; she has yielded this honor to her son. She has her own dwelling, that she may be to the right of her son.

MENEDEMUS: The right? With the son facing in which direction?

OGYGIUS: You are right to prod me: facing west, he has his mother on the right; facing east she's on his left. However, she doesn't dwell there yet because the building isn't finished and the place is quite drafty with the windows and doors open and the ocean, the father of winds, nearby.

MENEDEMUS: That's tough. Where does she live, then?

OGYGIUS: There is a small chapel within the unfinished building. It is constructed of wooden boards, and narrow doors on each side allow visitors to pass through. There is very little light, only as much as the candles provide, which give off a very pleasant scent.

Mary Shrine

MENEDEMUS: All this promotes a feeling of devotion.

OGYGIUS: Indeed, and if you looked inside, Menedemus, you would say that it was a dwelling fit for saints. Everything glitters with jewels, gold, and silver.

MENEDEMUS: You make me want to go there myself.

OGYGIUS: You wouldn't regret such a journey.

MENEDEMUS: Is there holy oil?

OGYGIUS: Silly question—only the tombs of saints exude holy oil, for example the tombs of Andrew and Catharine. Mary is not buried.[13]

MENEDEMUS: True. My mistake. But finish your account.

OGYGIUS: To spread the pilgrims more widely, different things are shown in different places.

MENEDEMUS: And also perhaps to encourage more generous donations, according to the proverb "The loot comes in more quickly when it is sought by many hands."[14]

OGYGIUS: And there are always custodians present.

MENEDEMUS: Are they canons?

OGYGIUS: No, canons are not used at all for fear that religious devotion might cause them to stray from their devotions. They might not take thought of their own virginity, while honoring the Virgin's. The only place where a canon stands by the altar is in the innermost chapel, the sanctuary of the Holy Virgin.

MENEDEMUS: What for?

OGYGIUS: To receive the offerings and to keep an eye on them.

MENEDEMUS: Are people pressured into making an offering against their will?

OGYGIUS: No, but when a person is standing by, a sort of pious embarrassment moves some people to make a donation who wouldn't give anything if there were no witness. Or sometimes they give more generously than they would otherwise.

MENEDEMUS: That's human nature for you. I know all about it.

OGYGIUS: In fact, there are some so devoted to the Most Holy Virgin that they pretend to place an offering on the altar, but instead by a surprising sleight of hand take what somebody else has placed there.

MENEDEMUS: And if no one were standing by—would not the Virgin strike them with lightning?

OGYGIUS: Neither the Virgin nor indeed the heavenly Father himself, whom men are not afraid to deprive of his ornaments, even if it means breaking through the wall of the church.

MENEDEMUS: I don't know which to admire most: the cockiness of these criminals or God's clemency!

OGYGIUS: To go on with the description: there is a passage on the north side (not of the church, don't get me wrong, but of the wall enclosing the whole area around the church), which has a small door, the kind of door you find in noblemen's gates, so that whoever wants to enter must first risk his shins and then must duck down.

MENEDEMUS: It certainly wouldn't be safe to charge after an enemy through this door.

OGYGIUS: Right you are. The sacristan told me that a knight once fled on horseback and escaped through this door from the hands of his enemy who was hot on his heels. In his despair he had commended his life to the Holy Virgin close by. His intention was to take refuge at her altar if the door was open. Now listen to the miraculous outcome: the knight suddenly found himself within the churchyard, while the other man was outside, raging in vain.

A sketchy miracle

MENEDEMUS: And they believe this wonderful story?

OGYGIUS: Of course.

MENEDEMUS: But a philosopher like you wouldn't accept it so readily.

OGYGIUS: The sacristan showed me a copper plate nailed to the door on which there was a picture of the knight who had been saved, dressed in the kind of clothes worn in England at that time, just as in old paintings, and if they don't lie, barbers weren't very much in fashion in those days, nor were weavers and dyers.

MENEDEMUS: How so?

OGYGIUS: The knight was bearded like a goat and his garment all of one piece and so tight it didn't have a crease. He was not a big man, but the tight garment made the body look even thinner. There was another plate, too, that showed the size and the shape of the shrine.

MENEDEMUS: So one could no longer doubt the story.

OGYGIUS: Below the little door there is an iron grating, so that only people on foot can enter. It was considered inappropriate that a horse should tread on the spot the knight had consecrated to the Virgin.

MENEDEMUS: And rightly so.

OGYGIUS: To the east is a chapel filled with wonderful things. I went there myself. Another sacristan received me. We said a short prayer and then were shown the joint of a human finger—the largest of the three. I kissed it and asked whose relic the finger was. "Saint Peter's," said the sacristan. "Not the apostle," I asked. He confirmed it. Considering the enormous size of the joint, which looked like it came from a giant's finger, I said: "Peter must have been an exceptionally large man." When I said this, one of my companions burst out laughing, which was annoying, because if he had kept quiet, the attendant would have kept nothing from us and shown us the rest. However, we appeased him as well as we could by giving him some coins. In front of the little building there was a covered structure. He explained that during the win-

On Relics

tertime, when everything was covered with snow, this structure had suddenly been brought here from far away. Protected by it were two wells brimful of water. They say that the spring is sacred to the Holy Virgin. It's a miraculous cure for head- and stomach ache.

MENEDEMUS: Who ever heard of cold water curing head- and stomach aches[15]—next they'll say that oil will put out fire.

OGYGIUS: My dear friend, we are talking about a miracle. If the cold water merely quenched men's thirst, there would be nothing remarkable about it.

MENEDEMUS: Obviously this is only part of the story.

OGYGIUS: They say that the spring shot up suddenly from the ground at the command of the Most Holy Virgin. So I inspected everything diligently and asked how many years it was since the little structure had been brought there. "Oh, centuries ago!" the sacristan said. "But the walls don't show any signs of age," I said. He didn't contradict me. "Even the wooden pillars don't look old," I said. They had been replaced recently, he admitted, and the fact was plain to see. "The roof, too, and the thatching of the dwelling appear to be quite new," I said. He agreed. "Nor do the beams and the rafters holding up the roof appear to be many years old," I said. He nodded. "But if no part of the original building has survived, how can we know for certain that this is the little building brought here from so far away?" I asked.

MENEDEMUS: And how did he manage to unravel that knot, I'd like to know?

OGYGIUS: He was quick to show us an old bearskin that was fastened to the pillars and practically laughed at us for being too dull to see such clear evidence. So we were satisfied and apologized for being so slow-witted. Next we turned to the heavenly milk of the Blessed Virgin.

MENEDEMUS: O Mother so like her Son! The son left us so much of his blood on earth; the mother left us so much of her milk. Yet it is hard to believe that the mother of an only child could have had so much milk, even if the baby hadn't had a drop of it.

OGYGIUS: They say the same thing about the Lord's Cross, bits of which are displayed in many places publicly and privately. If all the bits were brought together in one place, they'd be a load for a freighter. And yet the Lord was able to carry the whole cross.

MENEDEMUS: Doesn't that seem strange to you, too?

OGYGIUS: It might be called unusual, perhaps, but not strange. After all the Lord is omnipotent and can multiply these things at his will.

MENEDEMUS: That's a pious explanation, but I fear that many such things are devised for monetary gain.

OGYGIUS: I can't believe that God would permit men to mock him in this manner.

MENEDEMUS: But neither the Mother, nor the Son, nor the Father and the Spirit make the slightest move to frighten off criminals by a nod or a noise when they are being robbed by sacrilegious men. So great is the kindness of the divine.

OGYGIUS: You are right. Now hear the rest: The Virgin's milk is kept at the high altar. Christ is at the center and his mother (whom the milk represents) on his right.

MENEDEMUS: Is it clearly visible, then?

OGYGIUS: Yes, it's in a crystal container.

MENEDEMUS: A liquid?

OGYGIUS: Liquid? Go on! It flowed fifteen hundred years ago. It has congealed and looks like powdered chalk mixed with egg white.

MENEDEMUS: Why don't they show it without container then?

OGYGIUS: To save the Virgin's milk from being fouled by the kisses of men.

MENEDEMUS: You are right, for I think there are some who will kiss it with lips that are neither pure nor chaste.

OGYGIUS: When the custodian saw us, he came running up, donned a linen garment and draped a sacred stole around his neck, fell devoutly on his knees and adored the relic. Then he held out the holy milk for us to kiss. So we too kneeled devoutly on the lowest step of the altar. First we greeted Christ, then I said a short prayer to the Virgin, which I had prepared for the occasion: "Virgin Mother, you were thought worthy of nursing at your virgin breasts the Lord of heaven and earth. We pray that, cleansed by his blood, we too may obtain to that blessed and wise infancy which knows no evil, no fraud, or deceit, and forever longs for the milk of the gospel teaching until it progresses to perfection in the full measure of Christ, whose blessed company you enjoy forever, with the Father and Holy Spirit. Amen."

MENEDEMUS: A pious prayer, no doubt. What happened next?

OGYGIUS: Unless my eyes deceived me, both Virgin and Son signaled to me, for the sacred milk appeared to rise up and the monstrance shone a little more brightly. In the meantime the sacristan had come up to us and wordlessly held out a tray like the one used in Germany by those who collect tolls on bridges.

MENEDEMUS: I've often cursed those money-raking trays on my travels through Germany.

OGYGIUS: We gave him some money to offer to the Virgin. Then I put a question to him through a young man, whose name was Robert Aldridge,[16] if I'm not mistaken. He knew the language and was a smooth talker. I inquired as politely as possible how they could prove that this was the Virgin's milk. My motives in asking were pious. I wanted to stop the mouths of certain people who habitually laugh at all such things. At first the sacristan frowned and kept silent. I asked my interpreter to press him for an answer, but in even gentler terms than before. In fact he spoke so gently that even the Mother on her childbed could not have taken offense at being addressed in such words. But the sacristan stared at us as if stunned, and apparently horrified by our blasphemous question, expostulated with us. "What need is there to ask such a question," he said, "if you have an authentic plate commemorating it?" It looked as if he was going to throw us out for heretics, but an offering of coins mollified him.

MENEDEMUS: And what did you do next?

OGYGIUS: What do you think? We slipped away as if we had received a beating or been struck by lightning. We asked him humbly to forgive our bold question. For this is how one must act in sacred matters. Next we proceeded to the small building that is the Virgin's home. As we went in, the sacristan, a member of the Franciscan order, appeared and had a good look at us. A little further on we encountered another man who gave us the same attentive look, and after that a third man.

MENEDEMUS: Perhaps they wanted to make a drawing of you.

OGYGIUS: They gave me a different impression.

MENEDEMUS: What impression?

OGYGIUS: That some sacrilegious individual had stolen something from the treasure of the sacred Virgin and that the suspicion had fallen on me. Therefore I entered the shrine and greeted the Virgin Mother with this prayer: "You alone among women are both mother and virgin—most blessed of mothers and purest of virgins—we who lack purity come to you in your purity to greet you and to honor you as best we can with our petty gifts, so that your son will make us worthy of emulating your life, and through the grace of the Holy Spirit to conceive our Lord Jesus spiritually deep in our hearts and once we conceived him never to lose him again. Amen." And with these words I kissed the altar, laid down some coins, and left.

MENEDEMUS: And what did the Virgin do? Did she give you a nod or a sign that she had heard the prayer?

OGYGIUS: The light was dim, as I said, and she stood in the shadows on the right side of the altar. Moreover, the words of the last sacristan had discouraged me so much that I did not dare lift up my eyes.

MENEDEMUS: Then your journey did not have a very happy ending.

OGYGIUS: On the contrary, a very happy ending.

MENEDEMUS: That's encouraging, for "my heart had sunk to my knees," as Homer puts it.[17]

OGYGIUS: After a meal we went back to the church.

MENEDEMUS: That was courageous, considering that you were
suspected of sacrilege.

OGYGIUS: Perhaps so, but in my own eyes I was free of guilt. A
good conscience knows no fear. A desire to see the plaque to
which the sacristan had referred us drew me back. We looked a
long time until we found it posted very high up so that not every-
body was sharp-eyed enough to read it. My eyes aren't exactly the
eyes of Lynceus,[18] but then I'm not blind either. Aldridge read it
and I followed along more or less for I did not want to rely on him
in such an important matter.

MENEDEMUS: And were your misgivings completely cleared up?

OGYGIUS: I was embarrassed that I ever had any misgivings. The
matter was put so clearly: the name and the place was given, the
events related in order—in short, nothing was omitted. It mentioned a certain William, a pious Parisian, devout in many things
but particularly in searching all over the world for relics of the
saints. He had traveled through many regions, had inspected many
monasteries and churches until he finally came to Constantinople,
where his brother was bishop. When he was preparing to depart
again, his brother told him of a virgin consecrated to God, who
had in her possession the milk of the Virgin Mother. It would be
a great blessing, he said, if he could obtain a portion of the milk
by entreaty, money, or cunning. For the rest of the relics he had
collected so far were nothing by comparison with this sacred milk.
Hearing this, William had no peace until through entreaties he obtained half of the milk. With this treasure in his possession he considered himself richer than Croesus.[19]

MENEDEMUS: Of course he would. And it was such an unexpected
thing, too.

OGYGIUS: He immediately hurried home, but on the journey he
was laid low by illness.

MENEDEMUS: Such is man's fortune. It cannot be lasting or perfect.

OGYGIUS: When he saw that he was in danger, he secretly summoned a Frenchman, who had been a most loyal companion on

A Cock + bull story about how the milk got to England.

the journey. Swearing him to secrecy with a holy oath, he committed to him the milk on condition that on his safe return he should place the treasure on the altar of the Holy Virgin in Paris, where she dwelled in a great church that overlooks the Seine flowing by on both sides.[20] Indeed, the river appears to part in honor of the Holy Virgin. To be brief, William died and was buried, the other man continued on the journey. He, too, was seized by an illness, and despairing of life gave the milk to an English companion, obliging him with many oaths to do what he would have done himself. He died; the Englishman deposited the milk he had received on the altar in Paris, in the presence of the local canons who were at that time called "regular canons" (such as still live at St. Genevieve's[21]). He asked for and obtained from them half of the milk, brought it to England and placed it in the church by the sea, where he had gone on the inspiration of the Holy Spirit.

MENEDEMUS: The story certainly makes sense. ⌉

⌊OGYGIUS: Indeed; and so that there would be no room for doubt, the names of the suffragan bishops were added who granted indulgences[22] according to their authorization to those visiting the milk. And of course they asked for a small donation.

MENEDEMUS: What was the limit of their authorization?

OGYGIUS: Forty days.

Attack on me Treasury of Merits.

MENEDEMUS: What, are there days even in hell?

OGYGIUS: There is time at any rate.

MENEDEMUS: After they have dispensed their supply of indulgences, there are none left to grant, I suppose?

OGYGIUS: Not at all. Their supply is replenished. Their case is quite unlike that of the Danaids,[23] whose jar is continually being filled, yet remains forever empty. In the other case, even if you take away continuously, the contents of the jar never decreases.

MENEDEMUS: If a hundred thousand people are each given forty days, the number remains the same?

OGYGIUS: The same.

MENEDEMUS: And if those who received forty before lunch ask for another forty after lunch, there would be enough for them?

OGYGIUS: Even if they asked ten times every hour.

MENEDEMUS: I wish I had a chest like that at home. I would ask for no more than three coins, if only they would be replenished.

OGYGIUS: If you expect to receive that much in answer to your prayers, why don't you ask to be turned into solid gold?—But to return to the plaque. With a sort of pious candor this argument was added: The milk of the Virgin, which was being displayed in many other places, was certainly to be venerated, but the one here was more venerable than the rest, because the milk displayed elsewhere had been obtained from rocks, whereas this one had flowed from the very breasts of the Virgin.

MENEDEMUS: How could they be certain of this?

OGYGIUS: The nun who donated the milk said so.

MENEDEMUS: And perhaps it was St. Bernard who told her.

OGYGIUS: I would think so.

MENEDEMUS: For in his old age he had the fortune of tasting milk from the same breast that nursed baby Jesus. And I wonder why he is called "mellifluous" rather than "lactifluous."[24] But why would a substance that did not flow from her breasts be called milk of the Virgin?

OGYGIUS: Because it too flowed from her breasts, but it was scraped off a rock on which she happened to sit while nursing. It dripped on the rock, congealed, and by the will of God multiplied in this fashion.

MENEDEMUS: I see. But go on.

OGYGIUS: After we had read the plaque and were ready to leave, walking around a little longer to see if there was anything else worth seeing, the sacristans appeared again. They watched from the doorstep, pointed at me, drew near, then withdrew, rushed up again, nodded, and seemed to want to address me, if only they could screw up the courage.

MENEDEMUS: Were you not concerned?

OGYGIUS: On the contrary, I turned to them smiling and looking them right in the eye, inviting them to address me. Finally one of them approached and asked my name. I told him my name. Was I the man, he asked, who put up a votive tablet in Hebrew? I said yes.[25]

MENEDEMUS: Do you know Hebrew?

OGYGIUS: No, but they call anything they don't understand "Hebrew." Next the sub-prior of the college came, having been summoned I suppose. . . . He greeted me very civilly, telling me how many people had labored over the lines and tried to read them, polishing their eyeglasses in vain. Whenever some old doctor with a degree in theology or law arrived, he was immediately led to the plaque. Some said it was written in Arabic, others that it was a made-up alphabet. Finally they found a man who could read the caption. It was written in Roman capitals, he said. They were in fact Greek lines written in Greek capitals, which at first glance resemble Latin capitals. At their request I wrote down the meaning of the lines in Latin, word for word. When I repeatedly refused their offer of a small remuneration for my work, insisting that there was no work that I would not be most eager to do for the most holy Virgin, even if she ordered me to carry letters from there to Jerusalem —

MENEDEMUS: Why would she need you as a letter-carrier when she has so many angels by her side and at her feet?

OGYGIUS: —When I refused payment, the sub-prior brought out from his satchel a splinter of wood carved from a bench on which the Virgin Mother had reportedly sat. It gave off a wonderful scent which showed at once that it was a most sacred object. I prostrated myself, received this remarkable gift with my head bared, and in the greatest awe kissed it three or four times, and put it into my bag.

MENEDEMUS: May I see it?

OGYGIUS: As far as I am concerned, yes. But if you've already had your breakfast or if you had relations with your wife last night,[26] I would not advise you to look at it.

MENEDEMUS: No problem. Show it to me.

OGYGIUS: Here it is.

MENEDEMUS: Oh how fortunate you are to be the recipient of such a gift!

OGYGIUS: Just to let you know, I would not exchange this little splinter for all the gold in Tagus.[27] I'll have it set in gold, but in such a manner that it can be seen through a crystal. When the subprior saw me showing such devout joy in the gift, he thought I was worthy of having yet greater things entrusted to me, and asked me whether I had seen the secrets of the Virgin. I was somewhat awed by the word, but didn't dare to ask what he meant by the secrets of the Virgin. For in such sacred matters any lapse of the tongue can be dangerous. I said, no I hadn't seen them, but was very keen on doing so. I felt myself carried away as if divinely inspired. One or two candles were lit, and I was shown a small image that was neither remarkable for its size nor its material or artwork, but was very powerful.

MENEDEMUS: Size has nothing to do with working miracles. I saw a statue of Christopher at Paris.[28] It was bigger than a wagon, bigger than a giant—it was as big as a regular mountain, yet it was not known for miracles, from what I've heard . . . but go on with your account.

OGYGIUS: Next he showed us statues of gold and silver. This one, he said, is pure gold, this one is silver, gold plated. And he noted the weight and value of each statue and the donor's name. Marveling at each item in turn, I congratulated the Virgin on her blessed opulence. Our guide said: "I see that you are a pious sightseer, and so I think it is not right to conceal anything from you and you will see the Virgin's greatest secrets." At this he brought from the altar a wealth of wonderful things which it would take days to tell you about if I described them one by one. And so that journey came to a very happy end indeed. I had my fill of sights and I brought back with me that invaluable gift, a souvenir present from the Virgin herself.

MENEDEMUS: And have you put the power of your piece of wood to the test?

OGYGIUS: I have. Within three days I encountered in an inn a madman fit to be tied. The piece of wood was secretly put under his pillow, and he fell into a long and profound sleep. In the morning he rose sound in mind.

MENEDEMUS: Perhaps he wasn't a madman but merely a drunk. Sleep usually cures that illness.

OGYGIUS: If you want to joke, Menedemus, look for another subject. It is neither pious nor safe to joke about the saints. The man himself told me that a woman of remarkable beauty had appeared to him in his dream and offered him a cup.

MENEDEMUS: Of hellebore,[29] I should think.

OGYGIUS: We can't know for certain, but this much is certain: the man is sane.

MENEDEMUS: You didn't bypass the shrine of Archbishop Thomas of Canterbury?

OGYGIUS: Not at all. No journey can be more devout.

MENEDEMUS: I would like to hear about it, if it's not inconvenient.

OGYGIUS: On the contrary, I'd like you to hear it. The part of England that faces France and Flanders is called Kent. Its principal city is Canterbury. There are two monasteries there, almost side by side, both Benedictine. The one that's called St. Augustine appears to be the older one. The one that's now called St. Thomas appears to have been the Archbishop's see, where he lived with a few selected monks, just as today bishops have houses next to a church but separate from the houses of the remaining canons. For in former days both bishops and canons were monks, as historical evidence proves. The church consecrated to St. Thomas soars to the sky with such grandeur that it inspires awe even in those who see it from a distance. But its splendor darkens the glory of the neighboring buildings and overshadows the place that has been sacred from antiquity. The church has two huge towers that salute visitors from afar with bronze bells that give out a wonderfully deep sound and make the neighborhood ring far and wide. In the vestibule of the church, which is on the south side, are stone sculptures of the three knights who murdered the holy man with their impious hands. The names of their families are added: Tusci, Fusci, Beri.[30]

MENEDEMUS: Why are impious men honoured in this manner?

OGYGIUS: They enjoy the same honor as Judas, Pilate, Caiphas, and the cohort of wicked soldiers whose images you see artfully carved on gilded altars. . . . On the north side wonderful mysteries were displayed: a large number of bones, skulls, jaws, teeth, hands, fingers, and whole arms. We knelt down before them and kissed them one by one, and there would have been no end to the marvels had not the man who acted as our guide on the journey rudely interrupted the sacristan's desire to show us everything.

MENEDEMUS: Who was this guide?

OGYGIUS: He was an Englishman by name of Gratianus Pullus,[31] *Colet* a pious and learned man, but not as favorably inclined toward that aspect of religion as I would have liked him to be.

MENEDEMUS: Some follower of Wycliff, I suppose.[32]

OGYGIUS: I don't think so, although he did read his books, wherever he got them from.

MENEDEMUS: So he offended the sacristan?

OGYGIUS: The sacristan brought forward an arm that still had bloody flesh on it. Gratianus was too horrified to kiss it and *It's* showed his disgust even in his expression. Soon the sacristan put *wealth* his things away. Next we saw the altar table and ornaments, and then all the treasures laid up in the chamber under the altar. You would have thought the mendicants were Midases or Croesuses,[33] when you saw the mass of gold and silver.

MENEDEMUS: No more kisses here?

OGYGIUS: No, but another kind of desire touched my heart.

MENEDEMUS: What desire?

OGYGIUS: I was sighing because I had nothing comparable to these relics at home.

MENEDEMUS: A sacrilegious desire.

OGYGIUS: I admit that much, and I asked for forgiveness from the saint before I left the church. . . . Later on an unfortunate incident almost destroyed our bliss.

MENEDEMUS: What kind of misfortune—I'm waiting to hear the story.

OGYGIUS: My companion Gratianus showed no tact at all. He said a short prayer, then asked the sacristan who was accompanying us: "Tell me, good father, is what I hear true? Was Thomas very kind to the poor in his lifetime?" "Very true," said the sacristan. And he began to relate a great many stories about his acts of kindness toward the poor. At that point Gratianus said: "You don't think that the saint's attitude has changed, except perhaps for the better?" The sacristan said it hadn't changed. Gratianus rejoined: "Since then the holy man was so liberal toward the poor when he was still poor himself and lacked money for the necessities of life, do you not think he would be pleased now that he is so wealthy and needs nothing, if some poor woman out there whose children are starving or whose daughter's chastity is in danger because they have no dowry or whose husband is ill and destitute—if such a woman were to ask the saint's pardon and take a fraction of his great riches to support her family, taking it with his consent either as a gift or a loan?" When the curator gave no reply, Gratianus who is an impulsive man, said: "I am absolutely sure that the saint would take pleasure in the idea that even after his death his wealth could help destitute poor people." At this the sacristan knitted his brow, pursed his lips, and looked daggers at us. Undoubtedly he would have spat at us too and driven us out of the church with curses had he not known that we came recommended by the archbishop. Finally I somehow placated his wrath with soothing words, saying that Gratianus did not mean any of this, that he was joking as usual—and at the same time I put down some coins.

MENEDEMUS: I totally approve of your piety. But sometimes I do wonder how they can justify spending so much money on building churches, decorating them, enriching them, observing no end or measure. I admit that there ought to be substance and majesty in the sacred vestments, and the vessels used at Mass in church must have their dignity, but why must we have so many baptismal fonts, so many chandeliers, so many golden statues, and immense sums of money paid for organs? Nor are we content with a single organ. And why spend so much money on hiring noisy musicians, while our brothers and sisters, the living church of Christ, waste away from hunger and thirst?

OGYGIUS: Every pious and sensible man wants a limit to those expenditures. But it is excessive piety that has given rise to these faults, so that it deserves a favorable reception, especially when you think of the opposite fault in men who rob churches of their wealth. And money given to the church by princes and monarchs could be wasted on worse: gambling or warfare. And if you took anything away, you would first of all be considered sacrilegious, secondly the donors would shut their wallets, and on top of this, it would invite robbery. Therefore the church is the custodian rather than the owner of these things. And I would rather see a church splendid with holy furnishings than a mean and empty one, as some are nowadays, resembling horsestalls rather than churches.

Attack on Iconoclasm

MENEDEMUS: But we read that bishops were praised once for selling off sacred vessels to help the needy with the money.

OGYGIUS: They are being praised today, too. But praise is all they get; to imitate them is neither allowed nor desirable, I believe.

MENEDEMUS: I am keeping you from telling your story. I am waiting for the denouement of the play. . . .

OGYGIUS: We were led back to the sacristy. There they took down a chest covered with black leather. It was placed on the table and opened. Immediately we all sank on our knees and adored it.

MENEDEMUS: What was in the chest?

OGYGIUS: Bits of linen rags that showed obvious traces of muck. They say that the saint used them to wipe the sweat from his face or neck, to blow his nose, or any other such mean things to which the human body is subject. Here again my friend Gratianus failed to display tact. Since he was an Englishman and well known and a man of some authority the prior kindly offered him one of the rags as a gift, thinking that he was offering a very welcome pres-

Relics Again

ent. But Gratianus showed no gratitude at all. He touched the rag with every sign of disgust and put it back with contempt, puckering his lips as if to whistle. For that is their custom if something that must not be disdained offends them. I was alarmed, feeling both afraid and embarrassed. But the prior, who is no fool, pretended that nothing had happened and after offering us a cup of wine sent us on our way with friendly greetings. When we came to London—

MENEDEMUS: Why London, when you were already close to your own coast?

OGYGIUS: I was close, but I was more than happy to avoid it. It is more notorious for fraud and robbery than the Malean rocks[34] are for shipwrecks. Let me tell you my experience on the last journey across. Several of us were rowed from the coast at Calais to a larger ship. Among us was a young Frenchman, poor and with his clothes in tatters. They demanded half a drachma from him— that's how much they extort from each person for this short ride. He pleaded poverty. They made a joke of it and searched him. Pulling off his shoes, they discovered ten or twelve drachmas under the padded soles. These they took away,[35] laughing in his face and jeering at the wretched Frenchman.

MENEDEMUS: What did the young man do?

OGYGIUS: What do you think? He broke out in tears.

MENEDEMUS: Had they any authority to do this?

OGYGIUS: As much authority as those who rifle through passengers' belongings and snatch purses when they get a chance.

MENEDEMUS: I find it remarkable that they would dare to act in this manner before so many witnesses.

OGYGIUS: They act openly to give the impression that they are acting on authority. There were many onlookers in the larger boat, and there were several English merchants in the rowboat, but they complained in vain. They made a joke of it and bragged that they had caught out a wretched Frenchman.

MENEDEMUS: I would make a joke of crucifying those pirates!

[margin handwritten note:] The crimes perpetrated on pious travellers.

OGYGIUS: The coast on both sides is full of such men. I deduced from this how the lords would behave if the rascals took such liberties. After this experience I preferred the roundabout way to the shortcut. Moreover, just as it is easy to descend to the underworld but most difficult to return, so it is relatively easy to land on this shore, but very difficult to leave. Sometimes ships from Antwerp are waiting in the port of London, and I decided to venture the crossing with them.

MENEDEMUS: Does Antwerp have such wonderful sailors?

OGYGIUS: I admit, a monkey is a monkey, and a sailor is a sailor, but if you compare them with those others who have learned to make their living as robbers, they are angels.

MENEDEMUS: I'll remember it, if I ever have the urge to visit that island. But return to the account from which I distracted you.

OGYGIUS: As we were on our way to London, not far from Canterbury, the road becomes rather narrow and is lined with steep banks on both sides, so that one cannot turn off but has to go on straight by that road. On the left side there is a little almshouse for old people. As soon as the inhabitants notice a rider approaching, one of them runs out and sprinkles him with holy water, then he shows him the upper part of a shoe tied to an iron ring on which there is a piece of glass that looks like a gem. People kiss it and make a small contribution.

shake-down

MENEDEMUS: On that type of road I prefer an almshouse full of old people to a band of strapping robbers.

OGYGIUS: Gratianus was riding on my left, closer to the almshouse. He put up with being sprinkled with holy water, but when the man held out the upper part of the boot, he wanted to know the meaning of it. The man said it was the boot of St. Thomas. Gratianus said heatedly to me: "Do these beasts want us to kiss the boots of all good men? Why don't they hold out some spittle, while they're at it, or some other bodily excrement?" I felt sorry for the old man and comforted the poor fellow with a coin.

MENEDEMUS: If you ask me, Gratianus was right to feel angry. If the boot and sandals of St. Thomas were kept as monuments to *gross!*

his frugal life, I would approve, but it is impudent to obtrude soles, shoes, and thongs to be kissed.

OGYGIUS: To say the truth, it would be better if such things were not done. But if things cannot be corrected on the spot, I tend to look at the positive side if possible. I comforted myself with the thought that a good man is like a sheep, a bad man like a harmful beast. A viper cannot bite after it is dead, but it can infect a man with its stench and blood. A sheep, while it is alive, nourishes us with its milk, clothes us with its wool, and enriches us with its offspring. After its death it provides useful hides, and all of it can be eaten. In the same fashion, brutal men, who are devoted to this world, are troublesome to everyone while they are alive and a nuisance to the living when they are dead because of the tolling of bells, grandiose funerals, and sometimes even through the inauguration of their successors who exact new fees. Good men, on the other hand, are of great benefit all around. This holy man is a case in point. When he was alive he promoted piety by his example, teaching, and counsel; he comforted the destitute and helped the needy. And in death his usefulness is even greater: he built this rich church, he lent prestige to the clergy in all of England. And finally, he provides a living for an almshouse with this piece of his boot.

MENEDEMUS: This is indeed a pious way of looking at it. But I am surprised that a man of your cast of mind has never visited the cave of St. Patrick,[36] about which the people tell wonderful tales that are hardly believable.

OGYGIUS: The facts themselves are stranger than any fiction.

MENEDEMUS: Have you managed to see the cave, too, then?

OGYGIUS: I have sailed the Stygian Lake, descended into the jaws of Avernus[37] and seen the underworld.

MENEDEMUS: You would do me a favor if you told me about it.

OGYGIUS: This preliminary talk has been long enough, I think. I must go home and prepare lunch, I haven't had anything to eat yet.

MENEDEMUS: You haven't? For religious reasons?

OGYGIUS: No, out of spite.

MENEDEMUS: To spite your stomach?

OGYGIUS: No, to spite those greedy innkeepers who don't want to give you a decent dinner, but have no qualms asking the guest for an indecent amount of money. I wanted to avenge myself on them in this manner. If there is hope of a better meal with a friend or a more generous innkeeper, my stomach won't be able to stand lunch. But if good luck presents me with the kind of lunch I like, I have a stomach ache at dinner time.

MENEDEMUS: Are you not embarrassed to appear mean and stingy?

OGYGIUS: Menedemus, if embarrassment costs you money, it's a bad investment, believe me. I have learned to save my embarrassment for other purposes.

MENEDEMUS: I am keen on hearing the rest of your story. I'll join you for dinner, then we can talk at leisure.

OGYGIUS: Thanks for inviting yourself; others are in the habit of saying no when they are invited. And you deserve thanks twice over if you dine with me today, for I'll be busy greeting my family. I have a plan that's more convenient for us. Why don't you have me and my wife for lunch tomorrow? That way we can talk until dinner time, until you have had your fill. And if you want to go on, we won't desert you even at dinnertime. —Why are you scratching your head? Just prepare lunch and we'll come for sure.

MENEDEMUS: I prefer stories that come free of charge. —Well, all right, I'll give you lunch, but nothing very tasty unless you spice it with your tale.

OGYGIUS: But, tell me, are you not tempted to go on a pilgrimage yourself?

MENEDEMUS: Perhaps I'll be tempted when you have finished your story, but in my present position I am busy enough making the Roman rounds.[38]

OGYGIUS: Roman rounds? But you have never been to Rome.

MENEDEMUS: Let me explain. I make the rounds of the house. I go into the bedroom to make sure that my daughter's chastity is safe. From there I go to my shop and see what my servants are doing. Then on to the kitchen, where I check if anything needs correcting, and so on, checking what my wife and children are doing and making sure that everything is in order. These are my Roman rounds.

OGYGIUS: But St. James will take care of this for you.

MENEDEMUS: Scripture instructs me to look after these things myself. I have never come across a precept telling me to commit them to the saints.

NOTES

1. Translated from the Latin text in ASD I-3, eds. L.-E. Halkin, F. Bierlaire, and R. Hoven, 3 vols. (Amsterdam: North-Holland, 1972). An English translation of the complete colloquy can be found in *The Colloquies of Erasmus*, ed. and trans. C. R. Thompson (Chicago: The University of Chicago Press, 1965), pp. 285–312.
2. ASD I-3, p. 747.
3. Menedemus means "stay-at-home."
4. The name was probably meant to remind readers of Ogygia, the island on which the Homeric hero Odysseus was stranded for seven years.
5. River in the underworld; i.e., a rumor that he had died.
6. Menedemus is giving an exaggerated description of a pilgrim's outfit.
7. He is referring to the famous shrines of Santiago de Compostela in Spain and Walsingham in England.
8. The meaning is ambiguous. Menedemus uses "Greek" in the sense of either "pagan" or "esoteric."
9. A shrine near Basel.
10. Bede's epitaph is displayed at Durham, England. According to the thirteenth-century *Golden Legend* of John de Voragine, a message from God in answer to St. Giles' prayers was placed on the altar.
11. The Swiss reformer Ulrich Zwingli. In German "Ulrich" sounds like "Owl-rich," which is the meaning of the Greek composite Glaucoplutus. Zwingli advocated the removal of images from churches, a policy that was implemented by the town council of Zurich in 1524. The iconoclastic movement soon spread to neighboring towns.
12. Secular canons, unlike monks, did not take vows; regular canons lived by a rule, like monks.
13. According to Catholic doctrine, Mary, body and soul, was assumed into heaven.
14. Ovid, *Amores* 1.8.92.
15. In folklore cold drinks were held responsible for aches.

16. A Cambridge scholar (d. 1556) and a personal friend of Erasmus'.

17. *Iliad* 15.280

18. A mythological figure with penetrating sight.

19. Lydian king proverbial for his wealth.

20. Notre Dame.

21. Erasmus was familiar with this church because he had lived in the nearby Collège de Montaigu (now Bibliothèque Geneviève).

22. See above p. 44, note 10.

23. Their punishment in the underworld was eternal frustration. They were required to fill a leaky jar with water.

24. I.e., "Why he is called 'flowing with honey' rather than 'flowing with milk.' " St. Bernard was called mellifluous on account of his smooth style of writing.

25. An autobiographical touch. In May 1512 Erasmus announced his intention to visit Walsingham and to put up a Greek poem to the Virgin.

26. These prohibitions normally applied to people wanting to receive the host at Mass.

27. River in Spain reported to carry gold.

28. At Notre Dame.

29. Thought to cure madness.

30. A corruption of the names of the murderers Tracy, Fitzurse, and Le-Breton? Thomas Becket was murdered in 1172.

31. Pullus means "colt," i.e., John Colet (1467–1519), respected lecturer at Oxford and dean of St. Paul's in London, in whose company Erasmus made a pilgrimage to Canterbury.

32. Wycliff (1320–1384), declared a heretic by the Catholic church, also criticized pilgrimages.

33. Kings proverbial for their wealth.

34. A Greek promontory, proverbially diastrous to sailors.

35. Perhaps an autobiographical touch; when Erasmus crossed the channel in 1500, his money was confiscated by English customs officials. Their action was legal, however. Erasmus was not aware at the time that it was against the law to export currency.

36. In Ireland. It was thought to be an entrance to purgatory.

37. Entrance to the underworld.

38. A reference to processions making the rounds of churches in Rome during Lent.

BIBLIOGRAPHY

LITERATURE CITED

Allen, P. S., ed. *Opus epistolarum Des. Erasmi Roterodami.* 12 vols. Oxford: Clarendon, 1906–1958.

Augustijn, C. *Erasmus: His Life, Works, and Influence.* Toronto: University of Toronto Press, 1991.

Bezold, F. *Geschichte der deutschen Reformation.* Berlin: Grote, 1890.

Böcking, E., ed. *Hutteni Opera omnia.* Leipzig: 1859–1870. Repr. Aalen: Zeller, 1963.

Erasmus, D. *The Collected Works of Erasmus.* Toronto: University of Toronto Press, 1974 —.

———. *Erasmi Opera omnia.* Amsterdam: North-Holland, 1969 —.

Luther, M. *Werke.* Weimar: Böhlau, 1883.

Merker, P., ed. *Thomas Murners Deutsche Schriften.* IX. *Von dem grossen Lutherischen Narren.* Strassburg: Trübner, 1918.

Oxford Dictionary of English Proverbs. Oxford: Clarendon, 1970.

Ozment, S. *The Reformation in the Cities.* New Haven: Yale University Press, 1975.

Pastor, L. *History of the Popes.* 40 vols. London: Kegan Paul, 1913–1932.

Thompson, C. R., ed. and trans. *The Colloquies of Erasmus.* Chicago: The University of Chicago Press, 1965.

Walther, H., ed. *Lateinische Sprichwörter und Sentenzen des Mittelalters.* Göttingen: Vandenhoeck, 1966.

Whaley, D. *Later Medieval Europe.* London: Longmans, 1968.

FURTHER READING

Bietenholz, P., et al., eds. *Contemporaries of Erasmus: A Biographical Register of the Renaissance and Reformation.* Toronto: University of Toronto Press, 1985–1987.

Elliot, R. *The Power of Satire: Magic, Ritual, Art.* Princeton: Princeton University Press, 1960.

Frame, D. *François Rabelais: A Study*. New York and London: Harcourt, 1977.

Kaiser, W. *Praisers of Folly: Erasmus, Rabelais, Shakespeare*. Harvard: Harvard University Press, 1963.

Overfield, J. *Humanism and Scholasticism in Late Medieval Germany*. Princeton: Princeton University Press, 1984.

Screech, M. *Ecstasy and the Praise of Folly*. London: Duckworth, 1980.

Stokes, F. G., trans. *On the Eve of the Reformation: Letters of Obscure Men*. New York: Harper & Row, 1964.

Thompson, M. G. *Under Pretext of Praise: Satiric Mode in Erasmus' Fiction*. Toronto: University of Toronto Press, 1973.

INDEX